LEGAL PROJECT MANAGEMENT

CONTROL COSTS, MEET SCHEDULES, MANAGE RISKS, AND MAINTAIN SANITY

A DayPack Book

LEGAL PROJECT MANAGEMENT

CONTROL COSTS, MEET SCHEDULES, MANAGE RISKS, AND MAINTAIN SANITY

BY

STEVEN B. LEVY

A DayPack Book

2 4 6 8 9 7 5 3

DayPack Books   ●   Seattle, WA

For Miriam, Jeremy, and especially Anya, with gratitude.
Thank you for standing by me.

Table of Contents

Acknowledgments

There are so many people to thank. Alphabetically, thanks to...

- Monica Bay, editor of Law Technology News, for giving me chances to write and making me do so concisely.
- Scott Berkun, project manager extraordinaire and author, for his insights and encouragement. Go read his books.
- Mark Chandler, Cisco General Counsel, for being an inspiration to me personally as well as to an industry he's trying to reinvent.
- Paul Easton, project manager, whose web conversations were always stimulating, forcing me to test and challenge my assumptions.
- Ron Friedmann, colleague, for encouragement and belief that you can say project manager and lawyer in the same sentence.
- Kevin Harrang, colleague, for helping me bridge technology and law many years ago, and for being a terrific manager.
- Dr. Ted Klastorin, friend and author, for insights into project management and his allowing me to try out some of my ideas on his graduate students.
- Marc Lauritsen, colleague and author, for pointing me in the right direction and for a shared love of Shakespeare, whoever Will might have been.
- Aileen Leventon, colleague, for her many suggestions, her willingness to educate me, and her critique that resulted in a far better book than it otherwise would have been.
- Paul Lippe, the ultimate connector, for the way he puts both people and ideas together in exciting new ways.
- Jim Stanfill, co-worker, who taught me to manage smart, committed people by setting a clear vision and then getting out of their way.

Double thanks and an apology to anyone I've forgotten to name.

UP FRONT:

INTRODUCTION

All projects start with an Initiation stage.

(Even out-of control and unmanaged projects have an Initiation stage, though you might not notice it when everyone is flailing about.)

Here's the Initiation stage for this book.

Brief #1

About This Book

I'll to
my **BOOK,**
for yet ere SUPPERTIME
I must perform much **BUSINESS**.

Most projects fail.

Some fail outright. They are never delivered, or what is delivered is so far off the mark as to be unusable.

Others fall short – or, as the research organization Standish Group puts it with a delightful euphemism, they are "challenged." They fly high over budget. They fall disappointingly short in results. They take months – or years – longer than expected. Often, it's all of the above.

Some deliver but with ruinous nonmonetary costs. Team members aren't speaking to each other, vowing never to work together again – those that haven't left the organization outright. Trust between customer and supplier, client and law practice is irrevocably broken.

And some succeed. The percentage varies by industry, but in general only about one-third of projects are reasonably successful. The larger the project, the lower the success ratio.

Every successful project I know – those I've worked on, those I've studied, those I've observed or consulted to – has had one common thread. That thread is effective project management.

It hasn't always been "professional" project management. Smart people frequently can intuit the requirements of managing a project without formal training, often learning by observing others. There may not have been a designated "project manager." Always, though, there has been work easily identifiable, even in disguise, as project management.

Most cases or matters are projects, some small, some spanning years. Absent budget restrictions, you can work until you're done or the client is tired of paying... but budgets and limits are an increasingly prominent fact of legal life. And we all want our projects to succeed.

I am your theme; you have the start of me.
William Shakespeare, *The Merry Wives of Windsor*

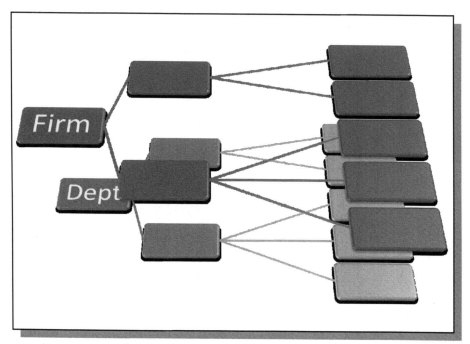

Who Is This Book For?

This book is for everyone considering or implementing Legal Project Management, LPM. (I recognize LPM = *Law Practice* Management for some.) My goals are threefold: help jumpstart a nascent field that can benefit everyone in the legal world; build a common understanding and shared vocabulary around LPM concepts; and offer a project management framework designed from the ground up for legal practices and attorneys rather than, say, engineering, construction, or IT.

Firm or In-House?

Most of the core concepts and execution of Legal Project Management are similar for firms and in-house departments. Where differences arise, such as the discussions of how the drive for billable hours affects projects or the distinction between issuing and responding to an RFP (request for proposal), I call out those differences explicitly. There is also value in firms understanding how in-house clients see cases as projects; likewise, in-house counsel can benefit from understanding how their firms manage these cases. If each party builds confidence in the methods of the other, it will be easier to reach fair and equitable agreements on projects that benefit both of them.

There is a brief at the end (p. 302) specifically for in-house departments helping their firms adopt and practice Legal Project Management.

Within the Legal Hierarchy

There are four significant Levels to implementing Legal Project Management, as described on p. 102:

- Level 1: Preparing the practice.

- Level 2: Training those who'll manage your legal projects

- Level 3: Deeply skilled Legal Project Management

- Level 4: "Accidental project managers" using the essentials of LPM.

Attorneys and other legal professionals who will be managing legal projects, or working on those managed by others, should focus on Levels 3 and 4, the *How* section. In particular, Level 4 is designed for the attorney who suddenly finds herself managing a project, the so-called "accidental" project manager (p. 106). Much of the How section of this book describes how to augment or tweak what you already know and do, applying it to managing legal projects.

Attorneys on the firing line can jump right in starting on page 18 and then move on to the How section starting on p. 113.

Practice executives and those focused on attorney development should focus on Levels 1 and 2: the *Why, What, Who, When,* and *Where* sections. LPM is a big change for most practices; mandates and memos work better when you prepare the ground as a change agent.

I'll to my book, for yet ere suppertime I must perform much business.
William Shakespeare, *The Tempest*

Why Should You Listen to Me?

I'm not a lawyer.

I'm a technologist and project manager turned businessperson. But I've spent a good part of my business career finding ways to make the legal process more cost- and time-efficient. I've driven tens of millions of dollars of cost out of legal systems. I've helped attorneys and other legal professionals become significantly more productive.

I've run my own business. I've run businesses inside one of the world's largest companies. And I've taught attorneys how to think like businesspeople.

I've managed multi-million-dollar projects to success in a number of areas. I've taken over and turned around projects that were failing, that were described as doomed.

I've led departments filled with hard-working, productive, and happy employees who sought opportunities to work for me again. As a business owner, a consultant, and a "go-fix-this" problem-solver, I've worked with clients and customers to understand what drives loyalty and satisfaction, and I've led work that improved both of these metrics significantly.

Throughout, I've been practical and pragmatic. I've learned to distinguish between what works and what only sounds good; I've always stuck with the former. In project management especially, there's a significant break between the two, the difference between striving to succeed and striving to not-fail.

Insanity and Project "Control"

Einstein supposedly defined insanity as doing the same thing over and over again and expecting different results. I've seen too much project management that Einstein would have called insane. Many project managers treat their *projects* as asylum cases, applying straitjackets and restraints to keep them under control. They never notice that they are neither delivering a cure nor preventing their patients from struggling.

Project control is no more project management than a TV's parental controls are effective child-rearing. Nowhere is that more true than in the legal world.

I'm not a lawyer, but I've worked with and supported lawyers for years. I deeply respect what they do, the skill with which they do it, and the intelligence and passion so many bring to their work. The emerging field of Legal Project Management is a practical tool not to constrain attorneys but to free them from the worries of project-managing complex cases so that they can better pursue the work that only they can do.

We could control them, if you would come to me.
William Shakespeare, *King Lear*

How This Book Is Organized

Every project tells a story.

They're true stories with many facets. The project manager is a reporter seeking the truth, trying to unearth it, finding and understanding the answers, searching for the stories behind the answers.

Who, What, Where, Why, When, and How

Reporters are taught to ask: Why, what, who, when, where, and how. To succeed at managing a project, you need to ask those same questions.

Because implementing project management – across a practice or even on a project already underway – is itself a project, I've organized the book according to those six reporter's questions.

Why should a practice bother with Legal Project Management? What's the problem LPM purports to solve? What's the case for LPM?

What is Legal Project Management *really* about? How is it different from traditional project management in ways that matter to law firms and in-house law departments?

Who should be involved with Legal Project Management? Who will make or break the initiative, both within and outside the project itself?

When should you implement Legal Project Management? How long does it take? How much time does project management itself take, and how much time and money will you save?

Where (in what environment) is the project happening? What is the practice environment?

How will you manage the work that surrounds and organizes the legal case (a/k/a project management)? How do you manage a project (case) to best support the legal work of the case? The *How* section is the longest in the book, containing detailed information for both accidental and specialist project managers. (By the way, many full-time project managers began "by accident," finding themselves managing a project without preparation or even intent. It's actually a great way to start.)

Beyond the Six Questions

Additional sections of this book describe the kind of training and coaching that can help a practice implement Legal Project Management; show LPM in the context of practice activities such as RFPs and fixed-fee billing; and provide further insight into tools and tips for managing projects. There's also a section for in-house counsel helping their outside counsel partners implement LPM, along with an index and extensive bibliography/reading list.

Let us from point to point this story know.
William Shakespeare, All's Well That Ends Well

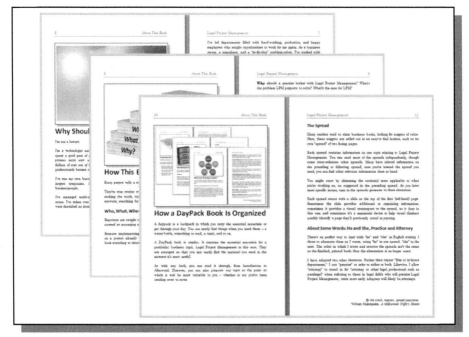

How a DayPack Book Is Organized

A daypack is a backpack in which you carry the essential materials to get through your day. You can easily find things when you need them – a water bottle, something to read, a comb, and so on.

A DayPack book is similar. It contains the essential materials for a particular business topic, Legal Project Management in this case. They are arranged so that you can easily find the material you need in the moment it's most useful.

As with any book, you can read it through, from Introduction to Afterword. However, you can also pinpoint any topic at the point at which it will be most valuable to you – whether or not you've been reading cover to cover.

The Spread

Many readers tend to skim business books, looking for nuggets of value. Here, these nuggets are called out in an easy-to find fashion, each on its own "spread" of two facing pages.

Each spread contains information on one topic relating to Legal Project Management. You can read most of the spreads independently, though some cross-reference other spreads. Many have related information on the preceding or following spread; once you've located the spread you need, you can find other relevant information close at hand.

You might start by skimming the section(s) most applicable to what you're working on, as suggested in the preceding spread. As you later meet specific issues, turn to the spreads germane to those situations.

Each spread starts with a slide at the top of the first (left-hand) page. Sometimes the slide provides additional or organizing information; sometimes it provides a visual counterpart to the spread, as it does in this one; and sometimes it's a mnemonic device to help visual thinkers quickly identify a page they'd previously noted in passing.

About Some Words: He and She, Practice and Attorney

There's no perfect way to deal with "he" and "she" in English writing. I chose to alternate them as I wrote, using "he" in one spread, "she" in the next. The order in which I wrote and rewrote the spreads isn't the same as the finished, printed book; thus the alternation is no longer exact.

I have adopted two other shortcuts. Rather than repeat "firm or in-house department," I use "practice" to refer to either or both. Likewise, I allow "attorney" to stand in for "attorney or other legal professional such as paralegal" when referring to those in legal fields who will practice Legal Project Management, since most early adopters will likely be attorneys.

By the scroll, masters, spread yourselves.
William Shakespeare, *A Midsummer Night's Dream*

About the Shakespearean Epigrams

What does Shakespeare have to do with Legal Project Management?

Nothing. And everything.

Shakespeare's plays had plans (plots), of course, though many were borrowed or adapted from earlier writers, such as Plautus (*The Comedy of Errors*). Most theater people will admit that plots weren't necessarily his strong point.

People were.

Shakespeare understood that theater was about people – the way they interacted, the way they thought, the way they planned and plotted, the way they fell in and out of love, even the way they spoke.

That pretty much sums up project management.

The plot – e.g., the plan and its execution – drives the play, but the value and strength come from the players and their goals.

Or maybe that's post hoc rationalization. Maybe it's just that I like Shakespeare.

My "Rules"

All of the epigrams are taken directly from the plays or poems with no omitted words, and with no changes other than spelling out the occasional shortened syllable such as i' (in), th' (the), and so on. I admit to changing the sense of some quotations by starting them "in the middle" or ending them early. Shakespeare didn't write literally about project management, so I've taken some liberties.

I have also taken a bit of license with the punctuation, usually to emphasize a point, but on at least one occasion because scholars are at odds about what punctuation Shakespeare intended ("We? Fail? But screw your courage..." from *Macbeth*). The published versions of Shakespeare's plays, the Quartos and First Folio, themselves punctuate almost randomly; neither spelling nor punctuation was consistent 400 years ago.

And though Shakespeare didn't write about project management per se, there are projects that run through many of his plays. Some work out, usually because of good planning and a clear sense of "Done," such as Richard III's capture of the throne. Others fail in laughable or tragic ways – e.g., the pick-up actors trying to stage *Pyramus and Thisbe* in *A Midsummer Night's Dream* or Hamlet's attempt to avenge his father's ghost.

Adherence to project management principles might have helped.

All the world's a stage.
William Shakespeare, *As You Like It*

WHY...

...USE LEGAL PROJECT MANAGEMENT?

The business of every case, every legal matter is a project.

All projects are managed in some way, consciously or not.

Conscious management is better.

Brief #2

Why Would I Use Legal Project Management?

> Prithee,
> be my **PRESENT PARTNER**
> in this **BUSINESS.**

"You come in here with a skull full of mush and you leave thinking like a lawyer."

So intoned Professor Kingsfield, in the person of the late, great John Houseman (*The Paper Chase*).

What does it mean to think like a lawyer? Specifically, what does it mean to think like a lawyer not about the law, or its application, but about the *mechanics of practice*?

What *should* it mean?

Let's start from three premises related to Legal Project Management:

- The *practice* of law is a business.
- A major business goal is making money for its stakeholders.
- Businesses make money by selling customers something those customers value.

There are lots of shadings, of course. Law can be a noble profession. Many-way partnerships have a very complex definition of "stakeholder." The relationship with "customers" is considered collegial, so collegial we call them clients. Nonetheless, these premises lead to two realizations:

- Efficiency that boosts profit is important to a business.
- Customers/clients drive the business, not the other way 'round.

Effective Legal Project Management supports these realizations. As such, it starts and ends with the client/customer.

In your practice, is "thinking like a lawyer" aligned with the customer? The Five Credos are the client-focused version of thinking like a lawyer.

Their business might be everything.
William Shakespeare, *Twelfth Night*

On the Line: "Ready! Fire! Aim...."

If you're a working "line attorney" in a busy practice, what's your day like? Does any of this sound familiar:

- The client isn't communicating well with you.

- When he does, he tries to micromanage your work.

- There's pressure to bill or charge back, but the client – or the practice's client manager – keeps writing off hours.

- You're doing everything you can, but the client seems vaguely unsatisfied with the work, or the outcome.

- Your end up with deadline pressure no matter how soon you start.

- You're uncomfortable talking about the cost of the work, unsure how to discuss financial matters in the context of the substantive issues.

If you're the client, is your life at all like this:

- You're frustrated when the practice does work without consulting you.

- It's not always work you'd have requested, yet you feel obligated – or pressured – to pay for it.

- Your input, especially into the deeper business issues behind the case, is ignored or not sought.

- You have shrinking budgets to live within and need fiscal certainty and predictability.

- You're worried that you won't get what you need on time.

- You're uncomfortable talking about the cost of the work, unsure how to discuss financial matters in the context of the substantive issues.

Two different constituencies, different perspectives, yet similar issues.

Enter Legal Project Management

Legal Project Management isn't just scheduling and organizing.

Scheduling and organizing are part of Legal Project Management. At least as important is the way LPM can increase communication by providing a structure for necessary but often omitted or awkward conversations – not just cost, but the range of outcomes, the business value of the work, the difference between needs and wants. These conversations take place between practice and client, within the project team, even with third parties.

If you're not communicating, you're shooting in the dark. It's pretty hard to hit the target you can't see, especially if it's a moving target.

To be successful, you have to take better aim at the issues you have in common, to shine a light on the systemic differences between client and practice, and to understand the divergence of goals across the team.

Ride upon the violent speed of fire; fly with false aim.
William Shakespeare, *All's Well That Ends Well*

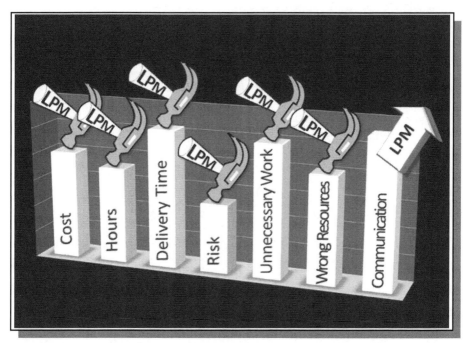

Why Legal Project Management?

Practices may recognize the need for Legal Project Management as they look to handle certain types of cases effectively.

Why Project Management?

How can a firm, say, feel confident about large fixed-fee cases without confidence in their ability to control costs on those cases? Even if you look at past average costs for such cases, at a minimum there will be worry about a new case blowing up both the budget and the average. And if the deeper goal is to increase profits, settling for average won't do; you need to aggressively control costs, respond to both expected and unexpected events, and do only the work that truly delivers value to the client.

The same holds for work taken on in house, though instead of profit the goal may be to do as much quality work as possible on your limited budget. Again, you need to control costs and manage surprises.

For both you gain predictability – of costs, of delivery dates, of results.

Not only fixed-fee or limited-resource cases benefit from Legal Project Management. Consider any case where you want to accomplish one or more of these goals:

1. Control or better understand the cost.

2. Control or predict the time spent, both cumulative time (hours) and running time (start to finish).

3. Be better prepared for events, especially unplanned events.

4. Deliver only the work necessary to meet the client's needs.

5. Engage the most appropriate resources to do the work best suited to them.

6. Improve communication on the team and with the client.

All the items on this list are goals of project management.

Why *Legal* Project Management?

For at least the near term, most legal projects will be led by legal, not project management professionals. Legal Project Management is designed for attorneys rather than project managers, taking account of the constraints surrounding both the practice and the business of law.

Also, the output – the deliverable, or "product" – of a case is significantly different from the output of standard project management – a construction project or piece of software, say. The different output and different processes require notably different techniques.

Ignorant what to fear, forced me to seek delays.
William Shakespeare, *The Comedy of Errors*

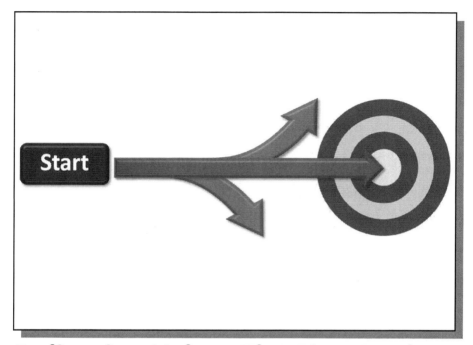

Delivering Value: The Five Credos

The focal point of Legal Project Management is the delivery of value, not just legal services. While "value" in that sentence implies value to the client, Legal Project Management also increases value for the practice.

In a firm, that value comes in the form of clearer control over profits and an increased ability to deliver the non-routine work that clients are willing to pay highly for. Don't forget that clients, no matter how much cost pressure they may be applying, need firms to be successful. They need to know that when they require specialized legal work, when there's a lot at stake, you'll be there to support them.

In house, that value comes from being able to deliver more and/or stronger legal services to the many corporate departments you serve. If budgets are flat or down and yet demands continue to increase, only through a rigorous focus on value-added legal work can you meet your corporate obligations.

Past Practice

Recall that Legal Project Management is not about the law but how you *work* on cases. As such, it goes counter to much of what attorneys have – and haven't – learned at law school and in the practice of law since getting that JD. We need new credos to replace today's mantras:

1. I do whatever it takes for the client.

2. I do whatever the client asks (if it's legal).

3. Partner profit is a function of one variable, hours billed.

4. I went to law school to practice law (and/or make a bunch of money), so don't give me that project-manager &@&(!(#!^.

5. I solve my client's legal problems, not business problems.

The third is firm-specific, but the others apply to both firms and legal departments. To some extent, clients have allowed these practices to take root and grow to full flower. If you don't ask how much it costs, or better yet tell the practice how much you think a matter is worth, then why shouldn't they pursue every thread, check every possibility? If you negotiate only hourly rates or hourly in-house chargeback fees, then the conversation is solely about money, not efficacy.

Practices have been responding by doing the obvious things, from cutting minor costs internally to delaying the hire of newly minted law-school grads to mass layoffs. Few of these thrusts will drive long-term profitability and stability the way Legal Project Management can: minimize low-value, off-center, or non-germane work; maximize efficient delivery of business value to client and practice through high-quality legal services; and minimize the impact of unplanned events.

Unquestioned matters of needful value.
William Shakespeare, *Measure for Measure*

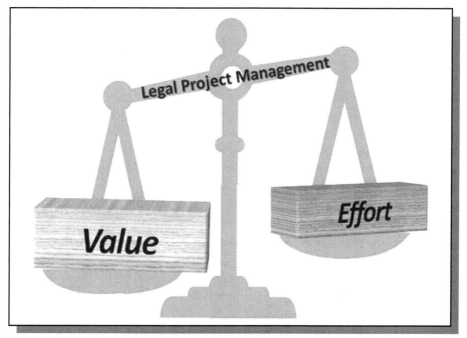

Credo 1: Work for the Client

The Old Mantra: I do whatever it takes for the client.

The New Credo: I will ask the client about their goal for this matter. I will ask what they and we need do to be successful, and what they would spend to achieve that goal. I will ensure that all work we do furthers that goal. I'll still do whatever it takes, but only on work that moves the ball toward the goal.

The client or corporation does not have a big pot of money into which the practice is entitled to dip. Rather, the client runs a business, a business with budgets and goals. Even individual clients have budgets and goals. Your job is to deliver *value* to the customer/client. Clients can no longer afford win-at-all-costs or exhaustive whatever-it-takes on every case.

The Value Equation

Value is an equation:

> Value = Benefit – Cost

Increase value by adding pure benefit, removing cost, or adding benefit that outweighs the cost. In other words, value is not independent of cost.

Sometimes the potential benefits of legal work are so high that cost becomes a small factor, such as in "bet the company" litigation. You'll know it when you're in such a situation, but most attorneys go their entire career without working on a Department of Justice v. Microsoft or Ernst v. Merck.

If a client considers a matter worth $10,000, don't spend $20,000 researching every last thread; it's not law school anymore.

How do you know what the matter is worth to the client? Ask!

Clients should tell you up front, but many don't. There is a certain squeamishness in talking money with lawyers (or doctors). Thus you, representing the practice, must take the lead and ask, "What do you expect to spend on this matter?" If instead the client asks *you* for a budget, prepare a reasonable one; then work to that budget. Sometimes extraordinary circumstances may require a budget adjustment; it happens in real life. Be honest with the client, and let them decide.

The In-House Counsel Version

Your business partners have budgets, whether or not you charge back. The GC certainly has a budget. Even if it's only corporate "funny money" (internal accounting transfers), the impact on the client's business is real. Work for the client.

> *Attorneys to their client woes.*
> William Shakespeare, *Richard III*

Credo 2: Own a Shared Goal

The Old Mantra: I do whatever the client asks. (I'll figure out if it's legal, first. Unfortunately, recent stories point out a few attorneys who forgot that part.)

> **The New Credo:** I will partner with the client to ensure we see the same goal the same way. If the client asks for work that doesn't support that goal, I will confer with the client before proceeding.

Projects often fail because of scope creep, an insidious expansion of the project's sub-goals. If your kitchen is torn apart amidst a remodel, why not add LED track lighting? It would look nice, and this is the time to do it. And afterwards, you'll wonder why it took longer and cost more than you expected. (Cool lights, though.)

In fact, most scope creep is less overt than the track lighting example. It's an extra bit of research. It's some new contract language "just in case." One more attorney present at a deposition. Legal Project Management helps guard against the seemingly minor tasks that cumulatively blow up the budget or the deadline.

Legal Project Management works only in the presence of Credo 2. If there's lack of clarity about the goal, every action becomes a question. Sometimes you need a specialist at a deposition, perhaps, or a particular clause in a contract. But how do you know for sure unless the goal is clear?

Client Confusion and Outside Counsel

Often a firm is engaged as outside counsel by a corporation's law department, but it's clear the work itself is for a particular (non-law) business inside the corporation. This situation is a recipe for either unhappiness or scope creep. The way to prevent such scope creep is to ensure that your joint goals are clear to the firm, the law department, and the corporate business you're serving.

When someone in that department asks for a particular service, compare it to the goal. If that service doesn't appear to support the goal, confer with the client (business and/or law department). Confirm that it's either a change in direction, with attendant consequences, or that you need to get back on the successful-outcome track.

The In-House Counsel Version

Use the client's annual goals and metrics, along with the matter's shared goals, to stay "on task."

In law departments that don't charge back, the client may think of your work as "free." People tend to consume excessive amounts of things they believe are free. This is one spot where it pays for the client to understand the practice's goals as well as you understanding theirs.

Good counselors lack no clients.
William Shakespeare, *Measure for Measure*

Credo 3: Participate in Profitability

The Old Mantra: Profit is a function of one variable, hours.

The New Credo: I am part of a business. My goal as a
participant in the business's success is to increase profit
by helping the business find new income and/or reducing
costs of earning it. Efficiency matters more than hours.

Credo 3 At a Firm

At many firms, partner profit depends on hours billed. Overhead is fixed;
you pay for office space whether or not someone is doing profitable work
within it. Each hour has costs but by and large represents money rolling
in. The more hours, the more profit.

This model does not serve the client first, and thus is under siege.

In a business, profit is an equation:

Profit = Revenue – Cost

Attorneys participate in the firm's success – often as a current or future partner – by increasing profit. They find new income or reduce the costs of earning it.

Legal Project Management helps attorneys do both. Clearly, if project management keeps delivery within budget, then removing those blindsiding costs adds to profit. However, Legal Project Management also focuses on delivering client value. A client who receives unmistakable value from a firm will place more work with that firm... which leads to more revenue and more profit.

Some attorneys are resistant to Legal Project Management because they perceive additional I-didn't-go-to-law-school-for-this focus on costs and budget. Most attorneys hope to make partner, whether in this firm or some future practice; help them understand that learning about "business stuff" now prepares them for the day when their own income will depend on that "business stuff."

Every actor in show business understands their profession has the word "business" in it. Attorneys need to be in "law business."

Credo 3 at an In-House Department

Even when hours aren't visible to internal clients, the business requires efficiency. If you don't charge back, the general counsel has a fixed budget for salaries and outside counsel; if you spend that money on client matter A, it's not available for matter B. And if you do charge back, you don't need me to remind you of the cost pressure from clients.

Employed you where high profits might come home.
William Shakespeare, *Henry VIII*

Credo 4: Practice the Business of Law

The Old Mantra: I went to law school to practice law (and/or make a bunch of money), so don't give me that project-manager &@&(!(#!^.

> **The New Credo:** The attorney shouldn't become a project manager per se. However, practical project-management techniques draw on and supplement what the attorney already knows. Legal Project Management helps the attorney easily incorporate these basic techniques into the practice of law.

Few attorneys would dispute that each case/matter is a project of sorts. There's a start, an end (usually), and a result. The issue isn't *whether* they want to manage these projects better; it's *how*.

Not just *how*, but *how much time*. There is a legitimate fear of spending more time jumping through project-management hoops and processes than they will save in the work itself.

What little attorneys have seen or heard of project management can be a turn-off. Their interface with IT-led or PMO-led projects often touches the "bureaucracy" of those projects without any exposure to the benefits those teams – and the business – receive.

The IT Project Management Model

According to a noted research team at the Standish Group, two-thirds of IT projects fail totally or in significant part.

If attorneys see IT as the model, why would anyone be surprised that the shibboleth of project management raises attorney hackles?

If Legal Project Management makes the firm more profitable but the attorney's job less fun, it will likely fail. In a law practice, the assets go home at night. When they come in the next day, it may well be to a different practice that makes them happier.

Therefore Legal Project Management must at least be neutral in its effect on the job, but grudging acceptance isn't the goal – especially since there is a cost of time and opportunity to learning the discipline. It must be seen as a boon, a benefit, a tool to increase efficiency while making the job itself more rewarding.

The In-House Counsel Version

Corporations generally have numerous process and project experts, from six-sigma champions to PMOs to continuous-improvement learning-organization specialists. Applied properly, all of these can add value in the corporate setting. However, be aware that they don't map transparently to legal work.

This business will raise us all.
William Shakespeare, *The Winter's Tale*

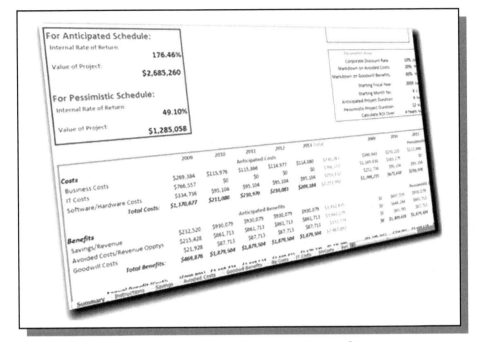

Credo 5: Clients Have Business Problems

The Old Mantra: I solve my client's legal problems, not their business problems.

The New Credo: My clients are businesses, and every problem is a business problem. I will use my legal skills to help the client strengthen the business, because that's the client's real goal, the true bottom line. I will remember that most clients not only are ethical themselves but understand that staying both legal and ethical is the best way to build a business and ensure long-term success.

Brad Smith, General Counsel at Microsoft, has a saying: "Don't tell clients whether they *can* do something; tell them *how* to do it legally." This is his way of getting in-house attorneys to partner with the business client, to help them solve their *business* problem.

(There are exceptions, though; it's awkward to describe a client facing incarceration as having a "business problem.")

Getting to the Business Problem

Attorneys involved in negotiating business deals see the business-problem aspect of law more clearly. Negotiations have a variety of potential outcomes, and the task is to obtain the best possible outcome for the client. To do so, the negotiator must understand the client's overall business goals.

Clients, trying to be helpful, often frame problems in a manner they think appropriate to their partner. They'll described desired technology or functionality to IT, rather than helping IT understand the business issue. Likewise, they'll frame a legal problem to an attorney; the attorney must understand the necessity of working back to the underlying business problem. Don't take at face value a client trying to speak your language; learn the client's language instead.

Consider: "I want to sue them." Why? "They're violating our patent." What's the impact? "We're losing sales to them." What do you want – their hide, or profit? "Profit, I suppose." And so on... with the alternative of a licensing deal now on the table.

Frame the business problem as a long-term (strategic) rather than near-term (tactical) issue. The actions you take may be tactical, but successful businesses focus on how actions play out over time.

This credo is the same **in-house** as it is at a **firm**.

Prithee, be my present partner in this business.
William Shakespeare, *The Winter's Tale*

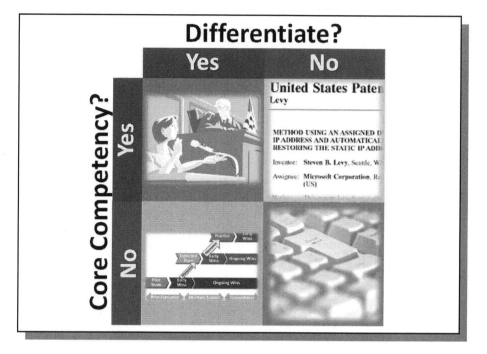

Core v. Context: A Case for LPM?

Are the tasks you undertake, as legal professional or project manager, core to your work and the practice? Do they differentiate you? Or are they commodity, the context for the truly important work?

Geoffrey Moore offers the idea of core tasks and context tasks. Core tasks are those specific and critical to the work you do; the rest is context. At a hospital, surgery is core, but the reception area is context. Context is clearly necessary... but you don't have to do it yourself. Indeed, there are businesses whose core is supplying receptionists. Your context can be someone else's core. Mark Chandler, CG of Cisco, takes core and context into a specific legal setting, crossing core and context with those things that differentiate you – as a practice or as a Legal Project Manager. See the slide above.

Consider a firm specializing in intellectual property. Their core competency is IP law. What differentiates them from other firms is their skill in licensing IP and, if needed, defending IP positions (upper left in the slide). While drafting patent applications is also core (upper right), it hardly differentiates them. Their ability to project-manage a patent case, whether through litigation or prosecution, also differentiates them via efficiency and cost control (lower left), but it's an adjunct to their core, not core itself. Finally, running an IP software solution is neither core nor differentiating (lower right), though they use such software.

They likely outsource the software already, licensing it from a vendor such as Anaqua. Drafting patents is likewise commodity; perhaps they train associates on this work, but they might outsource it to any of the hundreds of small-office and sole practitioner specialists in this field. Clearly they retain – and make the most profit from – protecting IP rights, though they might retain a local litigator, say, to front an East Texas court case.

That leaves Legal Project Management.

Who Will Do The Actual Legal Project Management?

That Legal Project Management is not a core competency but yet is part of what differentiates the firm suggests two options. First, the firm could bring in professional Legal Project Managers. Alternatively, it could recognize that some contextual work is so important to differentiation that it should remain in house; what you bring in is training and perhaps consulting, to create effective internal project managers.

Either way, a practice that recognizes Legal Project Management as important to future success must build or "buy" competency in the field. Project management of legal cases, other than perhaps e-discovery workflow, differs in many ways from project management in other fields. Thus Legal Project Management becomes an important competency to build and/or retain.

Call in the letters patent that he hath by his attorneys.
William Shakespeare, *Richard II*

Why Use Legal Project Management?

Prithee,
be my **PRESENT
PARTNER**
in this **BUSINESS.**

Brief #2

Checklist for Action

If your practice has these kinds of issues:

- *Cost overruns (or fear of cost overruns).*
- *Pressure to lower the cost of legal services.*
- *Poor communication with the client, or client dissatisfaction.*
- *Feeling that you're not in control of the case, or of the work surrounding the case (the "mechanics" of the case).*
- *Demands to improve profitability or do more with your budget.*

✓ *Learn more about Legal Project Management.*

✓ *Talk with colleagues who have implemented it effectively.*

✓ *Focus on the five credos.*

Key Takeaways

- Legal Project Management can help you:
    - Control or better understand the cost.
    - Control or predict the time spent, both cumulative time (hours) and running time (start to finish).
    - Be better prepared for events, especially unplanned events.
    - Deliver only the work necessary to meet the client's needs.
    - Use the most appropriate resources do the work best suited to them.
    - Improve communication on the team and with the client.
- Legal Project Management is based on but is different from traditional project management.
- Use the five credos to drive the delivery of business value to the client via the provision of legal services:
    - Credo 1: Work only towards the client's goal.
    - Credo 2: Partner with the client to understand the goal.
    - Credo 3: Participate not just in the work but in the profitability of the business.
    - Credo 4: Learn the techniques of Legal Project Management to more efficiently manage certain types of cases.
    - Credo 5: Use your legal skills in support of the client's business problems.

WHAT...

...IS LEGAL PROJECT

MANAGEMENT?

Ineffective leaders use "project management" as a shibboleth to fortify their position in an organization.

Good leaders recognize that project management can build stronger teams that deliver solutions with cost and deadline control and with improved communication all around.

Brief #3

What Is Legal Project Management?

> She promised
> and **ASSURED**
> **SUCCESS**
> in complete **GLORY**.

According to historian and author Michael Shaara's Pulitzer Prize winning book about the battle of Gettysburg, *The Killer Angels*, the turning point of the battle – and perhaps of the Civil War – was a failure of project management.

Of course, Shaara didn't call it project management.

On Day 2 of the battle, well into a hot July afternoon, General Longstreet, second in command for the South, orders General Hood to "take that mountain!" It's poor tactics, and Hood knows it. Hood offers an alternative plan. But Longstreet himself is under orders from commanding General Robert E. Lee to take the hill (Little Round Top) – despite his own misgivings, soon to be validated, about the wisdom of those orders.

Project management?

- Lee dictated tactics, not strategy, specifying them the night before.
- Longstreet couldn't meet Lee's timetable, taking hours to get into position. They apparently never communicated about the problem once Longstreet started moving his troops.
- When a worker on the project (General Hood) brought up not only a better solution but one that directly addressed the goal of getting around the Union flank and into their rear, Longstreet was unable to counter what he viewed as Lee's direct order.

Lee micromanaged instead of setting a clear vision – nowadays called the commander's intent – despite his hard-won knowledge that no battle plan survives contact with the enemy. There was poor communication even by 1863 send-a-rider-on-a-horse standards. They quickly fell behind deadlines but pressed on with the old plan anyway.

Good project management is designed to prevent this kind of confusion.

Take a trumpet, Herald. Ride thou unto the horsemen on yon hill.
William Shakespeare, *Henry V*

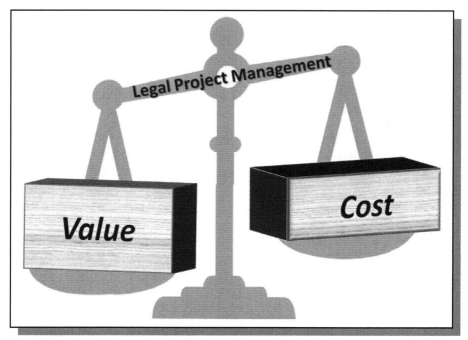

What Is Legal Project Management?

Legal Project Management (LPM) is the application of the concepts of project management to legal cases.

Legal Project Management, as an offshoot of traditional project management, is a new field. A number of practices are testing the waters, discovering that LPM is an effective way to control costs, deliver higher client value, work efficiently, and sometimes even find more enjoyment of the "real job" – being an attorney.

LPM is not about the *practice* of law, but about the mechanics of that practice. As such, it goes counter to much of what attorneys have learned at law school and later in the real world of firms, in-house departments, or even working for governments.

Building on Project Management Principles

Project management is defined by Wikipedia as "the discipline of planning, organizing, and managing resources to bring about the successful completion of specific project goals... while honoring project constraints." The Project Management Institute (PMI) definition is more formal and replete with buzzwords, but amounts to the same thing. Consider the key words and phrases:

- **Discipline** has dual meanings: Law is unquestionable a discipline requiring long study and practice, but being effective in both law and project management also requires self-discipline and focus.

- **Planning and Organizing** are the crux of traditional project management; they play a huge role in LPM as well.

- **Managing** inanimate resources – materials, for example – is much easier than managing the attorney resources of Legal Project Management.

- **Resources:** The majority of "resources" in many projects, including almost all legal projects, are people and time.

- **Successful Completion** is an obvious objective. In traditional project management, it's (usually) clear what successful completion means; see the next spread for what it means in the legal world.

- **Specific Goals** can define the difference between projects that work and those that never have a chance. Goal-setting is much harder than it may seem, because the players in a project are often aligned only superficially toward the same goal. See p. 154.

- **Constraints** usually involve schedules, the amount and type of work required, and resources.

I suspect this definition was written more by project managers than businesspeople. The business view of project management is a bit different – and the legal-world view is similar to the business view.

She promised and assured success in complete glory.
William Shakespeare, *Henry VI pt 1*

What's Different about LPM?

Let's take another look at that Wikipedia entry: "the discipline of planning, organizing, and managing resources to bring about the successful completion of specific project goals... while honoring project constraints."

One big difference in Legal Project Management is that the resources aren't always amenable to being planned, organized, or managed. Attorneys tend toward independence of thought and action; they're trained in competitive independence since law school. Time, in the form of schedules, is often set by others, from court calendars to clients.

Likewise, legal goals aren't always attainable, especially in adversarial situations. Missed goals would spell failure for, say, the project of constructing a house, but a legal *project* may be successfully executed even if the legal outcome isn't all that everyone hoped for.

Traditional project management is also – though not always – based on the idea that most work is fully controllable and predictable, if only you specify it well enough. In building a house, the architect and contractor know how much concrete they'll need for the foundation, how much roofing and sheetrock, and so on. They know how much sheetrock a carpenter can put up in a day, and how fast the painters can paint it.

Finally, where is communication in the Wikipedia or PMI definition? Communication is central to Legal Project Management.

Project Goals Are Business Goals

Legal Project Management views the practice of law in relation to business, whether the practice is a business enterprise in itself – i.e., a firm – or a department, a cost center, within a corporation. LPM has a relentless focus on delivering value, a ratio that includes cost and time, as well as delivering high-quality advice, documents, representation, and so on. It incorporates budgets and business constraints as well as schedule, scope, and general resource constraints. Legal Project Management recognizes the importance of effective communication to the predictable delivery of valuable work.

In addition, the real client often is not very knowledgeable about the legal work you're doing on her behalf. The business client, rather, has *business* goals. Much (not all) traditional project management unfortunately pays but lip service to business goals in favor of technical project goals, the equivalent of which in LPM would be legal goals.

Client legal goals can be simplistic at times. You're often providing legal services, either directly or indirectly through in-house intermediaries, to a business department whose leaders have little skill in legal matters. Imagine a client who commissions a new house from an architect by saying, "Create something nice for my family for $X and call me when it's done." Yet attorneys hear similar requests on a regular basis.

Aim better!
William Shakespeare, *Much Ado About Nothing*

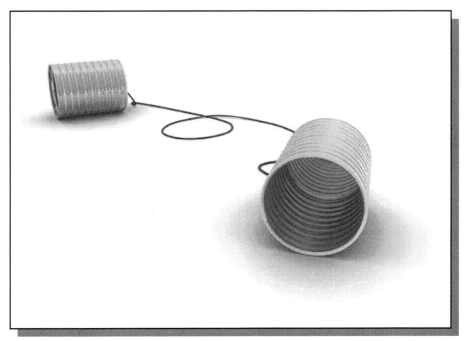

LPM and Communication

Legal Project Management can't by itself turn a poor communicator into a good one.

Good communication, however, means more than status reports delivered with monthly bills or chargeback statements. Legal Project Management provides a framework for such conversations. Without such a framework, they can be difficult conversations, with participants somewhat unsure of or uncomfortable with the grounds for the discussion.

Each of the areas listed on the opposite page fall within standard areas of communication, where LPM provides guidelines and guidance. Page references are to spreads in this book that detail the specific topics.

Structured Communication Topics

Business Problem: Legal Project Management guides the client and practice in talking in terms of the business problem (p. 154) underlying whatever legal work the client is requesting.

Short-Term, Long-Term: LPM ensures that discussions focus on strategy at least as much as tactics (p. 194), thus minimizing micromanagement by the client

Scope: Following procedures outlined Legal Project Management leads to discussion of and agreement on the *specific* work to be done, both breadth and the depth of the practice's legal work for the client (p. 173).

Budget and Fees/Chargebacks are often particularly difficult both for the attorney, who is practiced in legal rather than fiscal negotiations, and the client, especially a business client who may not understand the attorney's world. LPM provides a means to discuss budget openly and agree on the related tradeoffs (p. 162).

The Conditions of Satisfaction (p. 157) determine the extent to which the client is happy with the practice's work – which in turn heavily influences "repurchase intent" (p. 86), the likelihood of continued business from the client. LPM brings the conditions of satisfaction to the fore.

Stakeholders and Their Interests, especially hidden interests, can dramatically affect what seems like a straightforward project. LPM helps you spot hidden interests (p. 148) and surface or negotiate them.

Risks plague every project. You already know how hard it can be to state legal risks in a manner business clients understand. LPM provides a language for both legal and project risks, along with tools to help you track, mitigate, and respond to them (p. 184).

Speak, breathe, discuss.
William Shakespeare, *The Merry Wives of Windsor*

LPM and the Changing Law Practice

Practices are under pressure today. Clients demand a broader relationship. British attorney and writer Richard Susskind even calls the change "the end of lawyers."

It's won't literally be the end of lawyers, of course, as Susskind readily admits.

But it may be the end of business as usual.

Good legal service isn't cheap, and clients really aren't looking for Joe's Corner Legal Store and Bakery. They seek effective representation at a price they can afford. That's the business aspect of the law practice.

Smart practices are looking to Legal Project Management as part of a new approach to the business of law and the means by which they manage its time, money, and delivered value. To many, it's a road that's not on their maps, with unknown conditions ahead.

The road for many begins with an uphill climb. Attorneys don't want to be project managers... nor should they become project managers per se. However, if they learn to manage projects effectively and efficiently, they'll have *more* time rather than less to practice law, to do the work for which they sweated through law school and those first associate years.

Taking Care of Business

Like all good project management, LPM will help the practices that adopt it be more efficient and effective in reaching their goals and building a business model for the long term.

The law per se is not a business, but the practice of the law is. Law firms exist to make a profit, and law departments operate within strict budget confines – and both want to be successful enough to pay attorneys well and thus retain them in the practice. Granted, public interest law may be not-for-profit, but such practices usually operate so close to the bone that fiscal matters are at the forefront. Most government law groups, too, are strapped for resources; they too can use Legal Project Management to get the most value from those resources.

The practice of the "business" of law, whether in a standalone enterprise or within a larger entity, can use Legal Project Management to deliver heightened value. Calculating value includes cost and time as well as a focus on high-quality advice, documents, representation, and so on. Value takes account of budgets and constraints. LPM makes value predictable and repeatable.

Project management – legal and otherwise – approaches projects not with deep insight into issues of the law, or of the different ways of attaching roofing shingles through the underlayment. Rather, it focuses on the business-related aspects of projects – schedules, resources, cost, scope, communication, and delivery.

How the world is changed.
William Shakespeare, *The Comedy of Errors*

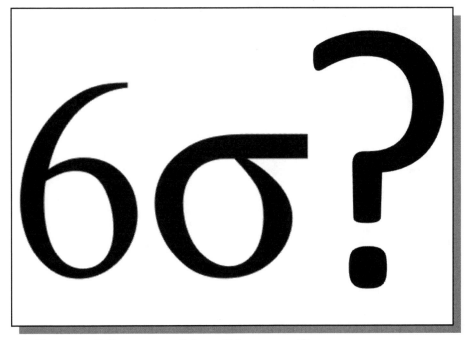

What About Six Sigma?

Six Sigma is a much-heralded methodology for improving repeatable processes.

It originated in manufacturing at Motorola, and was soon and famously adopted by Honeywell and then General Electric. More recently, there have been attempts to fit it to the practice of law, most notably at DuPont's law department, but also in house at Caterpillar and Motorola and at a few firms such as Seyfarth Shaw.

The Relationship of Six Sigma and Project Management

Six Sigma and project management in general share some characteristics that at first blush makes Six Sigma seem like a good match:

- A focus on predictable and repeatable processes.

- The importance of measurable financial return from implementing changes.

- The value of good metrics in ensuring that any movement is in the right direction.

- The significance of data as the foundation for decision-making.

However, Six Sigma also has a few critical characteristics that I believe are out of synch with the legal world:

- A heavy concentration on mathematical models to locate, define, and measure change.

- A separate structure of champions, black belts, green belts, and more that cuts across existing practice structures.

- Limitation to processes that can be exactingly measured, analyzed, and improved.

There is also a methodology called Lean, based on lean manufacturing concepts. Lean takes an approach to regularized quality improvement that is less constrained by mathematics, by manufacturing concepts (despite its heritage), and by fervid my-way-or-the-highway advocates. Lean and Six Sigma both derive from the same theories.

Lean has many aspects that can be applied easily and effectively to the legal world, meeting with less resistance than Six Sigma. There is also a movement to combine some of the best features of Six Sigma with Lean, called, appropriately, Lean Six Sigma.

I believe Lean Six Sigma has a lot to offer as an element of Legal Project Management – and that the essentials can be grasped rather easily. This book has a chapter near the end (p. 318) devoted to those essentials.

I have yet room for six.
William Shakespeare, *Antony and Cleopatra*

What About "Agile"?

So-called agile methods have had significant impact in the technology arena, an impact that will only continue to grow.

Defining Agile Methods

Agile methods attempt to improve predictability and deliver higher value by recognizing that most software development, in particular information technology (IT) projects, relies on broken communication channels – like the child's game of "telephone," where the first person (the customer or client) whispers in the ear of the second person. The whisper chain continues until the last person reveals what he has heard, which generally bears no relation at all to the original instruction.

Indeed, that scenario accurately describes *most* technology projects.

Traditional project management takes this bad communication as a given, requiring that everything be captured in great written detail up front, before any work begins, and that changes be highly restricted.

That manner of working is necessary on projects of such size and complexity that there are dozens of highly specialized roles, each of which can see only a tiny piece of the puzzle. On smaller projects, however, it may do more to protect the project manager than deliver value for the customer.

Agile methods developed as a response to the unwieldy structures of traditional project management. There are many agile methodologies, but they share a reliance on the ability of the project workers to act with intelligence and reason, a high degree of daily customer collaboration, and a recognition that change is the order of the day, especially since customers are better at defining what's wrong with their current solutions than creating a coherent and self-consistent picture of what they need. Thus agile methods rely on short, iterative cycles that deliver value with each cycle and build on learnings from the previous cycles.

Incorporating "Agile" Into Legal Project Management

I believe some agile principles play quite well in the context of Legal Project Management, although no one specific "agile" method maps cleanly to the legal environment.

Thus I've incorporated agile principles throughout this book without calling them out explicitly. Practical Legal Project Management, as explained in this book, utilizes rich communication with the client and relies on the intelligence and reason of the legal professionals working on the case.

There is no one formal, agreed definition of "agile." Anyone can call something "agile" – and someone else will argue with the definition's scope. That's another reason that I don't want to get hung up on labels.

His agile arm beats down their fatal points.
William Shakespeare, *Romeo and Juliet*

A Word on Electronic Discovery

Electronic discovery dominates many discussions of legal processes these days. E-discovery is also one place where project management is making significant inroads into the legal world.

However, e-discovery processes are more akin to traditional project management than Legal Project Management. There is an ever-changing set of e-discovery tools in use that incorporate many traditional project management techniques, in particular the idea of managed workflow.

The Outsource Model and Project Management

Consider that e-discovery is often outsourced, not just by in-house counsel to firms but by both firms and law departments to service bureaus specializing in e-discovery processes. Reviews of sensitive content and "hot documents," plus final reviews, are generally done by a case attorney, but the bulk of the process is managed by specialists.

At various points in the book, I explore potential areas where the legal project might be managed by professionals specializing in project management who may or may not be attorneys. While I don't foresee this situation occurring in the near future in most cases, e-discovery is one place where it *is* happening today. Project managers are managing not the evaluation of the content, which is of course a matter of law, but the workflow of collecting, storing, encoding, tracking, and producing thousands or millions of documents. That's a matter of project management.

Will the offloading of e-discovery process management to non-attorneys set a trend? Will it become a model for managing case-based legal processes? E-discovery supports standard project management because of its rigid and repeatable structure and because most of the hours are those of non-attorneys and junior attorneys. Few other cases follow this model. Even so, we as an industry can learn from watching the management of these processes.

The Cost Crunch and Project Management

The cost pressure in e-discovery is enormous. That pressure is recognized and accepted by almost everyone in the field – though some feel that the exceptions may be wearing judicial robes. Nevertheless, the incessant press of spiraling costs is forcing almost all of the parties involved in significant e-discovery to streamline their processes and focus on delivering the most value for the least cost in an acceptable timeframe. That's classic project management, and if you're not employing it on e-discovery, your costs are probably higher than they need be.

Perhaps the cost pressure isn't quite as extreme – or visible – on other matters, but it's still a factor. LPM can help relieve that pressure.

Bring forth this discovery.
William Shakespeare, *All's Well That Ends Well*

What Is Legal Project Management?

She promised
and **ASSURED**
SUCCESS
in complete **GLORY**.

Brief #3

Checklist for Action

If in addition to the checklist on p. 36 you want to improve communication between client and practice, Legal Project Management provides a framework for structured, effective discussions in the following areas, among others:

✓ *The client's business problem, not just legal issue.*

✓ *Long-term v. short-term or strategic v. tactical thinking.*

✓ *Scope – the breadth and/or depth of work the client seeks.*

✓ *Budget, fees, and chargebacks.*

✓ *Conditions of satisfaction and client long-term approval.*

✓ *Stakeholders – including hidden stakeholders – and interests.*

✓ *Legal, project, and case-related business risks.*

Key Takeaways

- Legal Project Management (LPM) is the application of specific principles of project management to the legal world.

- LPM streamlines and strengthens the business aspect of the practice of law – time, money, delivered value.

- You can't throw only traditional project management techniques at the problem; you need to understand how they play out in the context of a practice and modify them appropriately.

- Legal Project Management provides structures for improved communication between client and practice, including the discussion of uncomfortable topics.

- Legal Project Management is a good fit for the changes legal practices are facing.

- Some Lean and Six Sigma techniques can offer a useful adjunct to Legal Project Management, but they do not replace it.

- Much electronic discovery work, outsourced or handled by separate teams, is already using a traditional form of project management.

WHO...

...IS ON THE TEAM?

Soylent Green, according to Charlton Heston in the movie of that name, is people.

So is Legal Project Management.

It's a system, in part. It's an approach, in part. It's a set of techniques, tips, and tropes.

But most of all, Legal Project Management is the people who learn to practice the discipline.

Brief #4

Who Is on the LPM Team?

The mournful
CROCODILE,
with **SADNESS,**
snares relenting **PASSENGERS.**

In preparing for this book, I made a list of traits of project managers I've worked with. What traits did the good ones share? What about those whose name on a project roster would make me run the other way?

Before reading further, think about what qualities might be on that list. Being totally organized? Having a commanding personality?

Actually, both of those traits showed up more on the "avoid" list than in the "emulate" group. People who are tightly wrapped seem attracted to project management, but they're not necessarily successful at it, at least as I define project management success: projects deliver value, the project teams want to work with the project manager again, and that both of those statements remain true even in difficult situations.

What I found universal among the strongest players was caring about their team, the ability to retain a focus on customer/client value no matter what was blowing up around them, and a sense of humor. None were authoritarian. Not all were natural communicators, though they'd all achieved competence in that area. Some were organized, but a few appeared seriously disorganized – though even they could put their finger on any bit of project info almost instantly, meaning they organized their mental world rather than their physical surroundings.

But I keep coming back to the sense of humor. One project manager I respect was carjacked and taken hostage at gunpoint by a stranger. Within half an hour he'd talked the carjacker into letting him buy coffee for the two of them while they talked through the carjacker's issues. I asked him how he did it; he said he'd just looked for common topics they could laugh about, and he focused on the carjacker's needs rather than the immediate situation.

That seems like a model for resolving many project management crises too.

PS: Think twice before saying your project is "under the gun."

The humorous man shall end his part in peace.
William Shakespeare, *Hamlet*

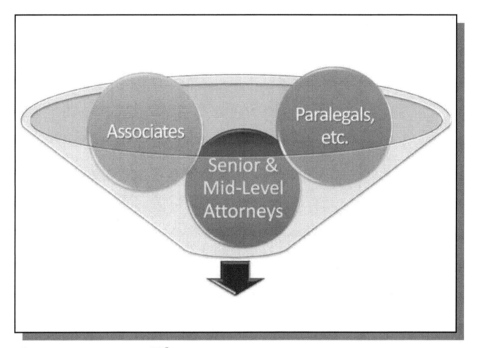

Attorneys First

Senior (partner) and mid-level attorneys are the likely initial cadre who will manage legal projects. They are the people you must win over first to the concept of Legal Project Management.

Job Satisfaction

Attorneys didn't go to law school to be project managers.

Except... they're project managers anyway. Every case, every matter is a project. Sometimes it's obvious: handling electronic discovery for a potential or actual lawsuit clearly looks and smells like a project, especially if you don't totally outsource the work. Sometimes the analogy is easily drawn: prosecuting a patent is a series of ordered steps. And sometimes it's cryptic: is giving legal advice a project?

It is important that the attorneys not view Legal Project Management as a burden, a hoop to jump through. It works best when they see it as an adjunct to their job, as a toolset that helps them work more efficiently.

Job Security

"Is Legal Project Management just a way to reduce the number of attorneys needed?" "How long before you 'offshore' the kind of work amenable to LPM?" These are legitimate fears, fears of the unknown. These fears might potentially be shared at all levels of the practice. However, those attorneys rising beyond second- or third-year associate status or the in-house equivalents are particularly at risk; they've progressed from work such as tell-me-what-to-do research into true knowledge-work artisanship and may unjustly fear LPM as a step back.

Influencers

Attorneys influence everyone else in a practice. You need them aboard the train, not grumbling about the coming of the railroad.

Who Will Do the Actual Legal Project Management?

Attorneys will lead most projects at most practices, at least until the discipline of Legal Project Management is more deeply established at that practice. Over time, paralegals or even professional "legal project managers" may handle project management for some types of cases.

By the way.... I asked on the facing page if giving legal advice is a project? If it's a one-time call or consultation, billed per hour, it's hardly worth considering a project. But what if there's research involved? What if those calls come regularly? (Especially for in-house counsel, calls add up quickly, and you need to regulate the time spent on them.) The moment you move from thinking only about hours to focusing on client value, you've got the makings of a project.

His former strength may be restored with good advice.
William Shakespeare, *Henry IV pt 2*

Spotting Likely Project Managers

As I noted above (p. 61), good project managers share various traits.

Collaborative – and care about their team: Legal Project Management requires collaboration, as detailed throughout this book. Many attorneys, however, have progressed by succeeding in competitive, non-collaborative environments. "Go it alone" and "my way or the highway" attitudes almost guarantee project manager failure.

Legal Project Management is more like a string quartet than an orchestra. There is no conductor; instead, usually one of the players also serves as leader, often but not necessarily the first violinist.

The project team may work under great stress, needing a significant amount of independent but focused action. Micromanaging such an ensemble will waste significant time in duplicative effort, failing to realize the time efficiencies of good project management. The best project managers not only respect their teams but care about their success as individuals on the project. They pull strong performances even from weaker or less knowledgeable members of the project team.

Hard to flap: Unflappability is great, but someone who recovers quickly from surprises can be just as effective. Surprises and bad stuff happen on projects. Look for attorneys who don't take changes in plan as personal affronts, whether those changes are mandated by the client or by circumstances.

Not afraid to communicate: If you can't deliver bad news and say "no" at times, the job's not for you.

Focus on customer/client value: Client value can't be an afterthought. The project manager up to her neck in alligators has to remember why she set out to drain the swamp. It's easy for goals-of-the-moment to usurp the project's overall goal. Good project managers find ways to keep refocusing themselves and the team on that overall goal (p. 160). Great ones never lose that focus in the first place, seeing every isolated piece in the context of the whole puzzle.

Not excessively risk averse: A project manager must be able to evaluate risk in context, not flee all risk. Becoming a project manager in a practice is itself a risk, the risk of trying something new.

Not full of themselves: A project manager is not a boss; don't get fooled by the second word in "project manager." (The discipline was probably named by someone with an inflated sense of self-importance.) Authoritarianism rarely works over the long term – especially when projects involve tradeoffs honestly made.

And... Don't Forget the Sense of Humor

The project manager who can't laugh at herself and at life's – and the project's – absurdities will struggle. Humor makes hard stuff easier.

The mournful crocodile, with sorrow, snares relenting passengers.
William Shakespeare, *Henry VI pt 2*

Finding the First Project Managers

Anyone with most of the traits in the preceding spread can become an effective project manager with training, coaching or mentoring (p. 294), and practice.

They may not become *great* project managers, but they can become *good*. Keep in mind that for most, project management will be their secondary job; they remain first an attorney on the case. (That said, it's possible that the occasional complex litigation, M&A case, or e-discovery process may benefit from a full-time project manager, a team member who – even if an attorney – is not really contributing to the *legal* aspects of the matter.)

Evaluate those traits, however, not in a vacuum but in the context of a project. For example, litigators cultivate a reputation for never being surprised – but some can be theatrical and controlling. Taking surprises in stride is a minimum criterion, but is not sufficient in itself.

Finding Initial Candidates in a Practice

Here are some things to look for in identifying attorneys within a practice for initial project-manager training and to become the practice's first project managers:

- The traits defined on the preceding spread.

- Willingness to try something new. They won't be "the expert," at least at first, nor will they necessarily have answers in hand to questions posed by the team or the client.

- An appropriate case at hand.

Unafraid of Looking "Foolish"

It's a tall order to ask of many attorneys: admit by actions and often words that you don't yet know what you're doing. It's like reliving the one-L or first associate year, or having the infamous "attorney's nightmare" – you're in court, you have no idea what the case is or even which side you're on, and you're probably naked to boot.

A Case in Hand

No two-hour or two-day or even two-week course – no, not even this book – can teach an attorney truly how to manage projects. Rather, courses or books prepare the ground, help them "know what they don't know," and, at least in the case of books, provide a reference resource to which they can turn.

What cements the training is being able to apply it almost immediately to a case to discover what the techniques look like in practice. Cases and coaches pave the road to success.

What foolish boldness brought thee to their mercies?
William Shakespeare, *Twelfth Night*

Overcoming Attorney Resistance

Resistance is likely on three fronts:

1. I am an attorney and I don't want to be a project manager.

2. Project management is a combination of process overhead and mumbo-jumbo.

3. I don't want to look or feel less than super-competent. (This last is whispered under the breath.)

I Am an Attorney, Not a Project Manager

Legal Project Management is not traditional project management. It utilizes the successful practicing attorney's current skills and knowledge. Attorneys already are project managers; they plan and organize cases and case strategy, they attend to client and fiscal matters, they have deliverables (which are not always documents; preparing a witness, for example, is just as much a deliverable as preparing a contract). Most of all, clients expect them to add business value through the provision of legal services.

If you're already doing it, why not learn how to do it better and with less struggle and pain? Remind them that Legal Project Management is not an outside discipline imposed on them, but rather a set of modified techniques based on work they're doing today.

Process Overhead and Mumbo-Jumbo

Unlike effective Legal Project Management, *bad* project management would have to plead guilty as charged.

That's why, throughout this book, I use either common-sense or legal-world terminology wherever possible. I introduce a handful of project management terms, but most – e.g., dependency – are the same as their everyday meaning. Even though attorneys understand more than anyone, except perhaps poets, the value of precision terms and language, I don't believe you need some Black's Project Management Dictionary.

Excess or obtrusive process overhead is a function of ineffective project management. It should be minimal in Legal Project Management, which is based on the work attorneys are already doing.

Feeling Less Than Super-Competent

Training and particularly coaching (p. 296) is the best way to help attorneys with this issue. You can assuage the fear somewhat, but effective coaching helps attorneys attain rapid competence in selected areas. On-demand coaching (p. 298) in particular drives both competence and confidence on tasks where attorneys feel the most pressure.

I decline; oh, train me not!
William Shakespeare, *The Comedy of Errors*

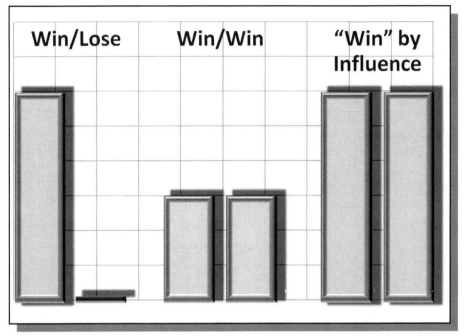

| Win/Lose | Win/Win | "Win" by Influence |

Harnessing Attorney Autonomy

People – attorneys especially – want autonomy over tasks that matter, as leadership guides Kouzes and Posner point out.

As I noted previously (p. 69), cynical attorneys may try to claim that Legal Project Management removes autonomy yet focuses on tasks that don't matter (a/k/a "paperwork," "process," timekeeping, etc.) The best way to get out in front of that attitude is to meet it head on.

Why Legal Project Management Matters to Attorneys

Attorneys need to understand why Legal Project Management matters – and believe it in their bones. They must know why it matters not (only) to the practice, but to *them*. How does helping the practice be more efficient help rather than vaguely threaten their jobs? How does better management of cases make their jobs better, especially those who are already expert at pushing routine and less-desired work to associates, paralegals, and secretaries?

Legal Project Management, properly implemented, will *increase* attorney autonomy. List Legal Project Management tasks for an attorney, and she'll realize she is already doing many of them – but in an unschooled manner. These tasks eat into her time, and into the extent to which she enjoys her work. She didn't go to law school to be a project manager, but she's doing it anyway, and doing it inefficiently – and likely ineffectively.

If that attorney can learn even a handful of tips, techniques, and tropes that will help her get on top of projects rather than be crushed under them, she'll feel better about her job. She gets to do more real legal work, and fewer project-based worries will follow her home at night.

You can tell her so, but it will be water off a duck's back. Instead, help her see it for herself. Offer examples. Point to the easy ways to improve these tasks in the "How" section of this book. Develop incentives to encourage her to try it, and to succeed rather than fight against it.

Don't turn it into a win/lose battle, or even try to find a win/win compromise. Instead, help her gain small project management victories that lead to no-compromise "wins" for both her and the practice.

Ensure that Legal Project Management becomes part of daily work, almost routine; she can't build confidence in a new skill set practiced but occasionally. Longtime attorneys Mark Young and John Gillies of Cassels Brock & Blackwell, studying knowledge management solutions, note that attorneys believe "tools should be worked into the fabric of their daily practice." That's how attorneys build confidence in their environment. What is demonstrably true for tools is equally valid for new procedures, new ways of thinking and working. Confidence counts.

Show boldness and aspiring confidence.
William Shakespeare, *King John*

Who is on the LPM Team?

The mournful
CROCODILE,
with **SADNESS,**
snares relenting **PASSENGERS.**

Brief #4

Checklist for Action

Here are recommended traits for a practice's first project managers:

✓ *They are willing to try something new and not afraid of looking slightly foolish when they do so. They are not trapped in their own egos.*

✓ *They care about people, especially the people on their teams.*

✓ *They aren't flustered when things don't go as planned.*

✓ *They're able to communicate bad news... and say "no."*

✓ *They live and breathe not only the law but client value.*

✓ *They have a sense of humor.*

✓ *The practice has cases ready for them to apply their new skills.*

Key Takeaways

- Attorneys are logically the first legal project managers in a practice.

- After a practice establishes routines around Legal Project Management, non-attorneys might begin to lead ("manage") particular projects. They would of course be leading only the project aspects, not the legal issues.

- A change agent has an insider edge... and insider blind spots.

- Legal Project Management can't be dropped on a practice, but must be organically integrated to the extent possible.

- You can facilitate change by influencing the players, especially the attorneys. You cannot mandate change successfully.

- The most effective project managers care about their teams, recover quickly when surprised, are not afraid to communicate bad news, focus relentlessly on client value, aren't self-important, and have the ability to laugh at themselves in public.

- You may have to overcome significant attorney resistance, usually around some combination of:

  - I don't want to be a project manager.

  - I'm not interested in more overhead or jargon.

  - It's important to me to at least look like I know what I'm doing.

- Don't turn implementation of Legal Project Management into a battle; it must be a partnership with the attorneys in which they can clearly see how their success benefits both them and the practice.

WHEN...

...DOES THE VALUE SHOW UP?

There are many synonyms for "hope."

Likewise, there are numerous synonyms for "new" and for "future."

One word is a synonym for all three: "Begin."

Brief #5

When Do I See Value?

Let's
ASSIST them,
for our CASE
is as **THEIRS**.

This brief is filed under its first word, "when," but the most important word is the last, "value."

"When" is easy. See the next spread, the shortest in the book. "Value" is a bit harder, because measuring it is particularly tricky.

I was once asked to survey and boost customer satisfaction for a product for which I was responsible. Of course I agreed; not only was a senior executive making the request, but it seemed a no-brainer that (a) customer satisfaction mattered and (b) we wanted it to increase.

Then our market research guru and I tried to figure out the details. Here are just a few of the issues we quickly discovered:

- Customer satisfaction (CSat) is a "downstream" metric, not something we could change directly. We had no funding to measure things we *could* change. (Consider a client relationship. You can change responsiveness, you can change fees, you can change attorneys, but you can't directly change "satisfaction.")
- The people who respond to a survey aren't necessarily representative; changing CSat for those with time and interest to respond might or might not change it for everyone.
- We had no proof that CSat correlated with increased revenue, which was the real goal. We both guessed they went hand in hand, but we had no way to test it on our limited research budget. The folks we really needed to understand were those who *weren't* buying the product, not those who were.

We eventually figured out a few things that "moved the needle," none of them learned through our surveys. I also learned how hard it really is to create metrics that accurately capture the data that *should* drive decisions. This brief describes those issues and how they apply to measuring value.

Direct my judgment. Let me see… I will survey!
William Shakespeare, *The Merchant of Venice*

When Should We Start Doing LPM?

Now.

(What are you looking for? There's nothing else to say on this topic.)

Start Today

Reading this book is a start, or, rather, a pre-start.

Start the real thing as soon as possible. (Or at least as soon as you have appropriate cases lined up.)

I remember now how he's employed. He shall in time be ready.
William Shakespeare, *Antony and Cleopatra*

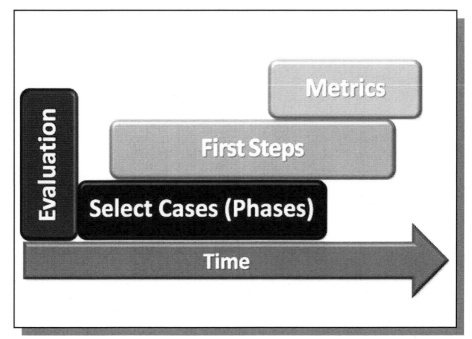

The Timing and Location of Value

Einstein said, "Not everything that counts can be counted, and not everything that can be counted counts."

Einstein's life's work was based on numbers, but he understood more clearly than most the limitations in mapping the rounded pegs of life into the square corners of numerical measures.

Legal Project Management is neither an overnight success nor a panacea.

The Time Factor

It takes time not just to train attorneys in Legal Project Management techniques but for them to begin applying those techniques fluidly to cases. Attorneys need to learn how to take depositions, properly word patent applications, file appellate briefs, or pretty much anything else they do. In training them, you recognize that there is a learning curve that kicks in after training; over time, they become efficient in these fields.

So it is for Legal Project Management.

Applicable Cases

The types of cases most likely to show *rapid* value involve regularized or repetitive work, such as patent prosecution, immigration applications, many types of contracts, quarterly corporate filings, and so on.

Consider also segments of large, complex matters that might be ripe for an early test of Legal Project Management. For example, much pretrial work, from responding to discovery requests to handling depositions, is somewhat regularized in structure.

Much of the work that gets "kicked downstairs" to, say, third-year associates could also benefit from Legal Project Management. The supervising attorney is already functioning as a type of project manager, delegating work and then checking the results.

You might also consider applying at least a veneer of project management to ongoing client communications (pp. 47, 156, 206). Building better relationships with clients via improved communication is one of the fastest ways of seeing value from your work in Legal Project Management.

Measuring Progress

The next sequence of spreads details the concepts behind honest metrics, along with pointing to ways to use them to measure a Legal Project Management program or LPM projects.

Let's assist them, for our case is as theirs.
William Shakespeare, *The Tempest*

A Brief Overview of Metrics

"Metrics" is a relatively recent business term referring to numerical data with which you can measure how well the business is executing against its goals. It sounds like a simple concept, but it's not. Unfortunately, many businesses use metrics simplistically; they are not a cure-all.

Why Measure?

The legal world has always used core fiscal metrics, whether firm profit per partner or departmental adherence to budget. Firms and some departments have also measured hours for evaluation purposes – i.e., in addition to the accounting required for clients. What more is needed?

Good metrics will tell you how efficiently you're meeting your core goals. Are you improving versus last year? Are some attorneys more effective than others, doing quality work in fewer hours? Do you have the right mix of attorneys and support personnel?

What are the metrics for success? More importantly, how do you know you've got the right metrics?

Can You Measure It?

One factor in defining a good metric is that it must be measurable. That seems like a tautology, a statement of the obvious, but consider: How do you measure attorney efficiency? Different clients have different demands. Different cases (usually) have different levels of complexity. If an attorney is assigned an ineffective researcher associate or paralegal, how much does that bear on your assessment of efficiency?

In cases such as attorney efficiency, you'll wind us using substitute metrics. These – and their perils – are described on p. 88.

How Do Your Metrics Relate to Your Goals?

Be sure you understand how the metrics you choose relate to your ultimate goal. Whether your "bottom line" is the literal bottom line of your financial statement or a measure of how well you serve your clients, map the alignment between metrics and desired results. The right metrics for a practice are those that drive desired behavior.

The Time Factor

Metrics measure differences – sometimes differences among attorneys, say, but more often they mark changes over time. For these periodic metrics, you need at least two measurements; metrics aren't a faucet you can turn on when you need water. Periodic metrics in particular are usually "longitudinal," comparing values over time rather than judging a single value against some absolute standard.

I am ill at these numbers.
William Shakespeare, *Hamlet*

Input v. Output Metrics

Economists love to tell the story of the Communist-era USSR screw factory. The USSR used "input" metrics, judging factory effectiveness by their monthly consumption of raw materials. Supposedly, on the first day of each month the workers at this factory would turn out a load of gigantic screws, and then take the remainder of the month off. By fully using their metal allocation, they hit their metrics. That no one needed these gargantuan screws wasn't their concern; it wasn't in their metrics.

Not all input metrics are bad, but none measure work produced, or value. For a firm, billable hours is an input metric. A firm can't use them up the way the screw factory tore through its allotment of zinc and steel, but neither do they correspond to what clients truly seek – advice, legal writing, filings, representation, and so on.

From the client's perspective, billable hours is a substitute metric (see p. 88). For the firm billing entirely or mostly by the hour, hours do map directly to the bottom line.

Input, Output, and Legal Project Management

The best project management focuses on output metrics – value produced, achievement of the desired result, and so on. Output metrics are those directly correlated with the goal, either profit or value. Profit is money received minus total cost to produce the work. Value is a bit squishier; think of it as utility to the "buyer" relative to costs, recognizing that we'd have to drag in too much economic theory and math right now to make it an actual calculated number.

The project manager also looks carefully at costs. For simplicity, consider cost a type of output metric. Unlike the screw factory's consumption, which bore no relation to useful output, costs correlate directly with a project's bottom line.

To produce profit or value, projects must control their costs. The largest cost is labor – the hours of the attorneys and staff. Thus the project manager wants to incur the lowest cost necessary to achieve output that meets the agreed quality standard – in other words, keep hours low.

Minimizing time spent is directly in line with an in-house department's goals and bottom line. However, it's 180 degrees opposed to the standard at many law firms, billable hours. Few attorneys consciously run up unneeded hours; nevertheless, the billable-hours metric exerts force in the wrong direction. Even if the firm is billing fixed-fee or other alternative arrangements, rating attorneys by hours worked is an input metric at war with the project's output metrics.

Overcoming the remaining tyranny of the billable hour can spell the difference between successful and unprofitable fixed-fee cases.

How may I do it, having the hour limited?
William Shakespeare, *Measure for Measure*

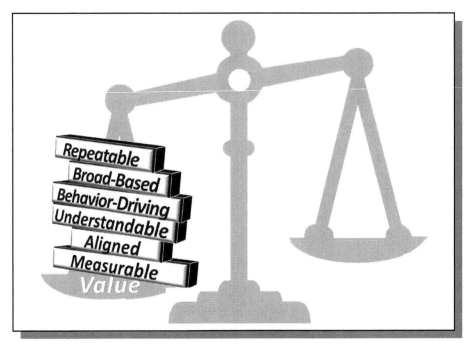

Defining Effective Metrics

The best metrics have the following characteristics:

Directly Measurable

We all strive for quality, for example, but it's not directly measurable. A manufacturing plant can track the number of defects per million pieces, for example, but a low defect rate is only one factor in defining quality.

Aligned (Cause-and-Effect) With Your Goals

The best metrics show direct cause-and-effect vis-à-vis your goals or bottom line. Correlation does not apply causation. (Suburban swimming-pool drowning *correlates* with ice cream truck visits, but there's no cause and effect; they're both tied to warm-weather behavior.)

For example, client satisfaction is a firm's substitute metric for what's known as "repurchase intention." It's good that the client is happy, but what really matters is her further use of your firm's services.

Understandable by Everyone in the Organization

If you're asking people to align to a metric, they need to understand it, and to comprehend the way their behavior influences the metric.

Drivers of Desired Behavior

Metrics can align with goals and yet not drive the right behavior. Winning in court is a desired litigation outcome, but consider a DA for whom percentage of court wins is a prime metric. Might he be tempted to prosecute only cases he knows he can win, plea-bargaining or dismissing the rest? Instead, the desired behavior should be getting and keeping the bad guys off the street – or, more cynically, getting reelected.

Good metrics measure or tie directly to specific behavior (actions) you can take to change them. Measuring, say, client satisfaction without understanding and measuring the things you can do that increase or decrease the metric is shooting in the dark.

For measurements of client-based data, the metric should be an *indicator* of desired *outcome*, such as repurchase intent.

Broad-Based

A profusion of numbers is confusing to those trying to meet them. A few metrics that provide reasonable coverage beats 50 perfect metrics.

Repeatable

In order to track change, you need to measure the same thing two or more times.

> *To vouch this is no test without wider and more overt proof.*
> William Shakespeare, *Othello*

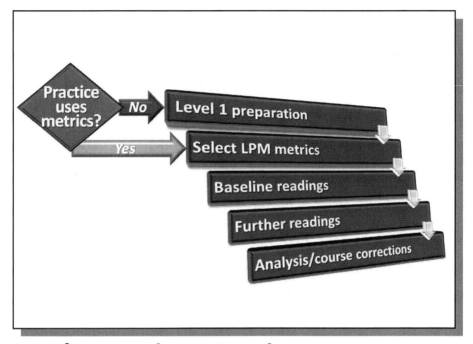

Implementing Metrics

Implementing metrics is itself a multi-tiered project. There is an "outer" project: moving the practice to a metrics-based "scorecard." Within that outer tier are small projects around the metrics themselves, either individually or in related groups.

Selecting LPM Metrics

There are three different groups of metrics within the implementation of an overall Legal Project Management program:

1. **Training:** How has the training and coaching program worked? Did you achieve expectations? How many attorneys have been trained? How many are still using LPM months after training?

2. **Individual Projects:** How will you measure specific projects
   (including those not otherwise taking advantage of Legal
   Project Management)? Adherence to deadlines? Meeting
   workload (hours) estimates? Client satisfaction? Attorney
   satisfaction?

3. **Business Results:** How will you determine the extent to
   which Legal Project Management is adding business value?
   This metric can be particularly difficult if you're using LPM
   to take on new types of business – e.g., venturing into fixed-
   fee waters for the first time. To what do you compare?

Getting Baseline Readings of Metrics

Most LPM metrics will be longitudinal (this time v. last time), to
determine how Legal Project Management is shaping projects and
improving the business of the practice. Thus you need to measure
starting points. Ideally, those starting points reflect the practice before
you begin Legal Project Management. However, don't use the lack of
baseline metrics as an excuse to delay an LPM program; instead,
measure progress against your early projects.

Getting Ongoing Readings and Adjusting Your Course

Once you've established a core set of metrics, let it become a practice
standard to re-measure at regular intervals – either on a calendar basis
for long-term work or at similar points in each project.

Metrics are meaningless unless you use them to spot areas where you
can improve – and then take steps to advance the practice. As part of
those steps, determine how much you'll expose particular metrics within
the practice. Even if you don't share *individual* progress or performance
metrics, I recommend you aggregate and share at least summaries.

Each day, say over the very same counting.
William Shakespeare, *Sonnet 108*

Substitute Metrics

Substitute metrics are the bane of any measurement regimen.

A substitute metric is one that measures not what you want to track but something you believe is *parallel* to it. For example, many businesses want to measure repurchase intent (p. 86), but that's hard to capture. Instead, they survey customer satisfaction, in the expectation that satisfied customers are more likely to use their services or product in the future.

However, a client can be very satisfied with you... but even more satisfied with a competitor. Or maybe they're looking for a less expensive option, or the person who specifies your services has changed, or external events are giving you a positive or negative aura unrelated to repurchase intent. That's the problem with a substitute metric.

Substitute metrics thrive on their convenience, not their accuracy.

Are Substitute Metrics Always Bad News?

Substitute metrics aren't bad per se; rather, you must treat them carefully, aware that they are not measuring the true goal. Don't get caught up in a scramble to improve your score on a substitute metric without trying to understand the differences between the substitute metric and the desired behavior.

The real danger is falling in love with a substitute metric and forgetting that it *is* a substitute. I've seen many companies do exactly that with the customer satisfaction metric; they lose awareness and early warning of customers who may be falling away for reasons unrelated to satisfaction.

Billable Hours

Billable hours, for a firm, is a classic substitute metric. Hours do not equate directly to overall profit, profit per partner or per equity partner, efficiency, productivity, attorney quality, or value of the work produced. What this metric has going for it is a wealth of historical data, its direct correlation with income (but not necessarily profit), how easy the data is to gather – and inertia. Everyone is accustomed to this measure.

LPM and Substitute Metrics

The biggest substitute-metric risk in standard project management is mistaking process compliance for actual results. A project that delivers the wrong output is of low value no matter how perfectly it's managed.

Processes themselves – LPM and otherwise – are in general substitutes for output. They're easy to measure, and in a lengthy project they may provide the only intermediate measures available. Well-managed processes may have significant value; however, the map is not the terrain.

Take convenient numbers.
William Shakespeare, *Coriolanus*

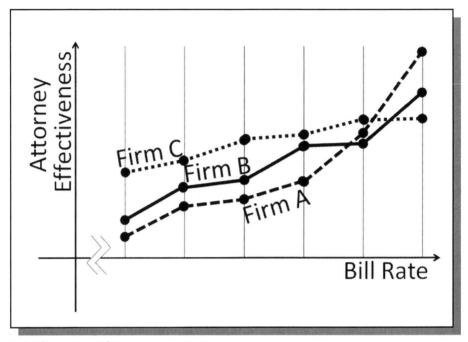

What Clients Measure

Different clients, of course, measure different things. In many cases, the metrics are topped by the substitute metric of client satisfaction (p. 90): as a client, how happy are we with the work done for us?

Here are some of the things that clients measure, according to a variety of recent surveys. (Most of these relate to firms, but some also hold true for internal clients evaluating service from their in-house counsel, especially those that charge back for legal support).

- **Total billing across all firms.** Bottom line: clients have budgets, and corporate budgets are promises, not estimates. When cost centers in particular exceed their budget, managers are at severe career risk. If budgets are tight, work will be cut – and that work might be yours.

- **Total billing per practice area:** Individual practice areas usually have sub-budgets; under budget pressure, a client may choose to deemphasize one area in favor of another.

- **Total billing per firm:** More and more clients understandably expect larger discounts from firms with which they spend the most money.

- **Attorney bill rates** comparing not just average rates per firm but the rates of, say, fifth-years at one firm v. those at a competitor.

- **Billing errors** as revealed by invoice routing and approval systems.

- **Satisfaction,** the all-purpose substitute metric. It's subjective... but it matters. It matters a lot.

- **Compliance with outside counsel guidelines** (not an actual number, but a factor in retaining a firm nonetheless).

- **Predictability,** the extent to which a practice meets expected spend and deadlines. There's a gotcha here – many clients are uncomfortable discussing these metrics up front... but nonetheless retain a mental picture of what they expect. It's hard to meet a metric you can't see; practice self-preservation, and solid project management, by asking up front.

- **Case resolution costs,** whether these come out of the law department budget, a business budget, or special one-time allocations.

- **Value** – still very subjective, but clients are starting to seek ways to make this metric more objective, given its importance.

Here are two difficult metrics that clients are beginning to wrestle with:

- **Efficiency/return on investment:** What do we actually get for the money we spend with firm X? How does that compare to firm Y?

- **Attorney effectiveness:** How "good" is a particular attorney? Is that partner really worth $1500/hour? Do we need a New York firm, or can we go to Bozeman, MT... or even Bengaloora (Bangalore), India?

We number nothing that we spend for you.
William Shakespeare, *Love's Labors Lost*

When Do I See Value?

Let's
ASSIST them,
for our CASE
is as **THEIRS**.

Brief #5

Checklist for Action

A good metric has the following characteristics:

✓ *The item is directly measurable.*

✓ *It is aligned with your goals in a cause-and-effect relationship.*

✓ *It is understandable throughout the practice.*

✓ *It drives the desired behavior.*

✓ *It is repeatable – you can measure the same thing at different times to track improvement.*

In addition, a few broad-based metrics are better than too many specific ones; people can focus on a limited number of targets.

Key Takeaways

- Metrics are critical to evaluating not just managed projects but a Legal Project Management program itself.

- Picking the right metrics is critical... and harder than it looks.

- The wrong metrics will drive behavior in unproductive directions.

- Beware substitute metrics in particular.

- Good metrics are directly measurable, aligned with your goals, widely understood within the practice, drivers of desired behavior, broad-based, and repeatable.

- You need to start sometime; start by getting baseline numbers. Unless they reveal immediate problems, use the changes in results over time to analyze and adjust your course.

- Your clients – most of them, anyway – are already using metrics to measure your performance as a legal practice, especially in the case of in-house counsel sizing up outside counsel. You need to understand what they're measuring in order to improve on your current numbers... because your competitors are out there promising to improve on *your* numbers.

WHERE...

...DOES LPM FIT IN A PRACTICE?

Have you noticed how few pools have diving boards these days?

Of course you noticed; you're an attorney, and you know exactly why they've been removed.

But then you're not one of those people who would dive in before checking to see if there's water in the pool.

Brief #6

Implementing Legal Project Management

Go
WITH ME, and be
not so **DISCOMFITTED.**
Proceed in **PRACTICE.**

Many claim that fish are unaware of the water in which they swim. In what do *we* swim?

Humans have had a sense of air since ancient times, believing it one of the four classical elements – earth, water, fire, and air. Yet it took a long time to build a real understanding of the "element" surrounding us. Oxygen, for example, wasn't indentified until the late 18th century.

What about organizations? In what element do they exist?

Organizational systems have been studied for little more than 100 years, and we continue to learn more each year about how they operate. Most of that knowledge is held by organizational consultants and specialists in organizational design. However, there truly are no secrets, no special club to join, no passwords, no initiation.

Blow on your hand, and you can feel the air around you. Move fast enough, and you'll feel the air's resistance.

Move fast enough in an organization, too, and you'll feel *its* resistance. Legal practices, shaped more through their history and traditions than fiercely competitive business pressure, are particularly resistant to change. In the law, slow change is good, but the principle of *stare decisis* may better serve the law than it serves the organizations that practice law.

Legal Project Management represents an overturning of precedent within most practices, a revision in the natural order to many attorneys. It can enter an organization in many ways, often slipping in when it's applied to a particular case.

One-project-only work styles, however, can make the practitioner feel like a fish out of water. Extending Legal Project Management effectively across a practice is easier when you understand the element in which it exists.

The motion of all elements courses as swift as thought.
William Shakespeare, *Love's Labors Lost*

The World Turned Upside Down

"Great," you say. "Let's start managing projects. Where do we start?"

Of course, you can start by picking specific cases or phases of cases (p. 81), by jumping right in with a bit of coaching (p. 296) or training (p. 290). Some practices will thrive on this approach, while others may do better with a formal program that includes broader training. However you approach it, think about how it fits the broader practice structure.

Techniques: Level 4

One way to get started is to help the "accidental project managers," attorneys who either recognize that they're managing project or who have been told to "project manage" a case (p. 106). They can learn to manage risk, make better plans, perhaps get a bit more predictable with delivery times. These aren't trivial benefits, but they're limited, hard to repeat and harder to extend systematically to others in the practice.

Projects: Level 3

Projects – managed cases – and the techniques for managing them are the end point, but they're not a broad-based starting point. Individualism, whether individual cases or individual attorneys, balances implementation and progress on the smallest blocks in the organizational system. It's easy for that system to become unbalanced, for the larger pieces piled atop the smaller to come tumbling down. It might not be a dramatic collapse, but it's an unstable arrangement nonetheless.

People: Level 2

Cases are led by people, project-managed by people. Without proper preparation, the attorneys and other legal professionals with significant roles on the case will have at best a patchwork structure to support them when projects under pressure develop the inevitable problems.

Legal Project Management training and coaching make up this block in the stack. Effort spent training the attorney project managers clearly provides a more stable base for the blocks. As valuable as a training program may be, a practice can create an even more durable foundation.

The Organization: Level 1

Organizational systems – the way an organization's structure guides the actions and reactions of its participants – are the foundation for lasting change, no matter what the organization. Organizational dynamics are complex, however; they're not well modeled by a series of small-scale interactions. Practices may not need organizational consultants per se, but modifying the system provides the broadest base for Legal Project Management success.

This house is turned upside down.
William Shakespeare, *Henry IV pt 1*

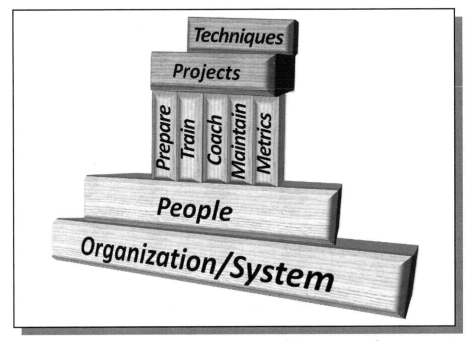

Levels 1 and 2: Foundational

If you're able to build from the bottom up, the strongest foundation upon which to implement Legal Project Management is an understanding of your organizational system.

Level 1: Preparing the Organization

If you understand your organizational system, you can influence it. If you influence it, you can tune it so that the system's "immune system" will embrace rather than try to reject your injection of Legal Project Management. (Never underestimate the power of system antibodies to reject change.) Champions within the organization – so-called change agents – can use a combination of system-change techniques and a strong training and coaching program to ensure that a new way of working takes hold.

The Five Credos (p. 22) are part of the foundation, framing the need for Legal Project Management as integral to the business and mechanics of practicing law. Consider questions such as these:

---

1. Why does the practice want Legal Project Management?

2. Who in particular wants it? What are their goals? To what extent will they stand behind these efforts?

3. How will they — and you — sell it to the legal practitioners?

4. Do you understand who the influencers are? The snipers? How do you win over the former and disarm the latter?

Change must be led, not mandated, at Level 1 by those who influence the system (p. 108) – the overall practice or a particular practice group.

Level 2: Training and Coaching

The building blocks of Level 2 support long-term success at Levels 3 and 4, the management of individual legal projects. There are five facets:

---

1. Preparing the attorneys to understand practice rationale and goals for Legal Project Management.

2. Training the attorneys via a formal, defined program that's really itself a project (p. 288).

3. Ongoing proactive and on-demand coaching (p. 296) to lock in and build on the gains of training, especially when the real-world projects aren't easily mapped to the training exercises.

4. Maintaining and sustaining the program to ensure it becomes part of practice culture.

5. Measuring the success of the overall program, not just individual projects (p.294).

If I mistake in those foundations which I build upon, the center is not big enough.
William Shakespeare, *The Winter's Tale*

Levels 3 and 4: Practical

In day-to-day Legal Project Management, the attorney-project manager takes control of the non-legal aspects of the case. While it's great if you can institute LPM on a case at the very start, you can bring a project manager aboard at any time. Use Legal Project Management to manage and oversee variables such as these that govern those agreements:

- **The "Done" statement**, a clear definition of successful outcome. What does the client need? What does the practice need? Are these needs aligned? And what does "concluded successfully" really mean when so many legal outcomes are gray rather than black or white?

- **Value**, the focal point of work for the client, Deliver increased value while lowering your costs of producing that value.

- **Expectations:** The client has certain expectations, whether or not she expresses them explicitly. You need to take those expectations into account in structuring the case, or risk "winning" the case yet having a client who, seeming inexplicably, is less than thrilled with your work.

- **Costs and budgeting:** Costs are what you spend to produce value, budgeting how you manage and account for those costs. Costs are usually measured in money and/or time.

- **Fees or chargebacks** are what the client pays for the value you deliver. (Not all in-house work has chargebacks.)

- **Deadlines:** When is the client expecting various work items from you? When can you deliver them? What are you telling the client about delivery dates? What other deadlines are in play, such as court dates or Rule 26 meet-and-confer needs?

- **Scheduling** arranges the work to add up to those deadlines.

- **Resource allocation:** Who will do what on the case? How do you get the right resources at the right time... and right cost?

- **Dependencies:** "For want of a nail...." Schedule dependencies, resource dependencies, other-party dependencies, work-product dependencies – manage them proactively, or fail.

- **Risks:** LPM helps you achieve success with both planned and unplanned events.

I've glossed over a whole lot of nuances. What happens when the client calls or Emails and says, "I need you to start work today on...?" Is a successful conclusion in, say, litigation the same thing as a courtroom victory? The How section goes into detail on these and other nuances.

To be honest, there's a certain amount of CYA ("cover your...") in the mix. But CYA is already happening with or without LPM. The good news is that when the attorneys apply LPM there's much less need for CYA.

Go with me, and be not so discomfited. Proceed in practice.
William Shakespeare, *The Taming of the Shrew*

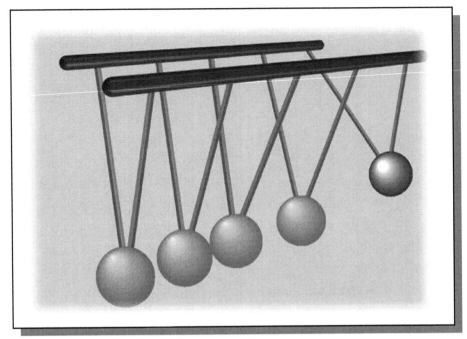

Level 4: The Accidental Project Manager

None of the truly outstanding project managers I know started out as a project manager. They didn't major in project management in college. Some had a mathematics or science background, but others studied fields as apparently unrelated as drama or theology. (Actually, I can see how both directing plays and serving as parish priest could be useful backgrounds.) Most became "accidental" project managers. Many moved back and forth over the years between project management and other careers.

On the other hand, I've known some truly ineffective project managers who came to the discipline by accident, and never got close to mastering it. And then two of the *least* effective project managers I've worked with *did* come out of college seeking careers in project management.

Being an accidental project manager can be a noble calling. Many accidental project managers first step up when they realize their project is failing because of poor planning, lack of communication, disorder, disorganization, unclear or conflicting goals, and so on.

What Does It Take to Succeed?

It takes three things to succeed:

1. An aptitude for project management – a sense of humor, controlled ego, a people focus, communication skills, a belief in value over process – the skills noted on p. 64.

2. A proactive willingness to take on the challenge.

3. A supportive environment.

A supportive environment is not just a practice that provides appropriate training and coaching when needed, but one where practice management recognizes the learning curve and understands that not everything the novice project managers does will be successful. A supportive attitude from practice management will also go a long way toward creating a supportive team – and a team pulling together is half the battle.

Note that being organized is not dispositive for project management success. An attorney who is intensely organized but who is a poor communicator will have a tough time as a project manager.

Likewise, an attorney uncomfortable with responsibility is a poor candidate. Project managers have to make tough decisions based on incomplete information. Some attorneys are unwilling to move until they believe they are in possession of *all* the facts. While a project manager should certainly strive to collect as broad a base as possible for decisions, often timeliness will outweigh completeness. Attorneys who flee such situations will rarely succeed at Legal Project Management.

The day was yours by accident.
William Shakespeare, *Cymbeline*

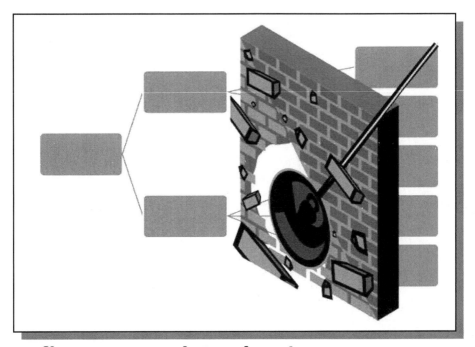

Influence and Authority

Managers exert authority.

Leaders extend influence.

Influence goes a lot further than authority. It goes down a lot smoother, too.

In a large corporation, influence is an executive's primary tool. In a law practice, extending influence is even more important – especially if you want to introduce or further Legal Project Management.

If you're the key influencer – say, a managing partner – then you probably already "get it." You've learned what battles you can fight successfully.

If you're not, though, you're going to need your influencing skills to cause a practice-wide rather than individual shift towards Legal Project Management. Even attorneys who see the need for LPM will be resistant. They want to practice law, not project management – and they're too busy for all that Legal Project Management nonsense anyway, right?

Whom do you need to influence?

1. The attorneys in your early-adopter group.
2. The legal professionals who work for them.
3. The management structure – managing partner, partner committee, etc.
4. IT, which thinks it's the last word in project management (and, in their defense, some IT teams do a very good job in managing computer projects).
5. The PMO (Project Management Office), if you have one, because applying standard project-management techniques unvarnished to a broad group of attorneys is rather like trying to give a cat a bath.

Bathing Cats

How *do* you give a cat a bath? One method involves heavy gloves, a long-sleeve shirt, and a significant tolerance for pain and blood. Another is to put the cat out in the rain (or a warm shower) for a bit and then let that sandpaper tongue take over.

It's difficult, and probably counterproductive, to *force* Legal Project Management on the attorneys in some way. Rather, lead them to it by using your influence. While negotiation is a factor in influencing others, it is not at all the same thing. A negotiation leaves everyone mildly happy; negotiators talk win-win, but I'm-okay-you're-okay is the norm. Use influence, not just negotiation, to make Legal Project Management a factor in your practice.

Words cannot carry authority.
William Shakespeare, *Henry VIII*

Implementing Legal Project Management

Go
WITH ME, and be
not so **DISCOMFITTED.**
Proceed in **PRACTICE.**

Brief #6

Checklist for Action

If you're considering

- *Bringing in training for Legal Project Management, or*
- *Implementing it in a practice-wide rather than on an individual per-case*

then:

✓ *Prepare the attorneys to understand practice rationale and goals.*

✓ *Train the attorneys via a clearly defined program.*

✓ *Add proactive and on-demand coaching to lock in and build on the gains of training.*

✓ *Maintain the program to ensure it becomes part of practice culture.*

✓ *Measure the success of the overall program as well as individual projects.*

Key Takeaways

- The platform for implementing Legal Project Management in a practice consists of four levels:

    - Level 1, System: How you influence the way the organization itself operates.

    - Level 2, People: How you help attorneys learn Legal Project Management.

    - Level 3, Projects: The individual cases and books of cases to which you'll apply Legal Project Management techniques.

    - Level 4, Techniques: The tools, techniques, and tropes of Legal Project Management.

- Legal Project Management can be practiced by both professional and "accidental" project managers.

- Accidental project managers may in fact perform quite well in managing projects, especially when supported by the organization.

- Organizational support includes not just training and coaching but an environment that sets reasonable expectations for the novice project manager.

- You can move an organization further by influence than by authority.

HOW...

...DO WE ACTUALLY DO IT?

Is project management hard?

Sometimes. But recovering from mismanaged or unmanaged projects is much harder.

Brief #7

LPM: Doing What You Already Know

To climb
steep **HIILS**
requires SLOW PACE
at **FIRST**.

Shortly before 8PM one autumn evening, I was standing on the corner of 57th St. and Seventh Ave. in New York City. A man came up to me and asked, "How do I get to Carnegie Hall?"

You know the old joke, right?

Except that the man was dressed in a tuxedo, carrying a violin, and looking rather worried. So I bit my tongue – how often in real life do you get handed a straight-line like that? – and pointed to the elegant building across the street.

There are likewise two ways to become a project manager. One is the same as the answer to the joke: Practice. Study, practice, learn, practice some more.

The other is to dash across the street, or take the subway, or do whatever you have to do to get there, to get on a project, to learn on the job. (And *then* practice, study, learn, and practice some more.)

Is it better to go through considerable training first? Sure. You can't just pick up a violin and expect to sound like Paganini. But what if you already know how to play the viola? You still won't sound like Paganini, with your awkward fingering and on-the-fly intonation adjustments, but you'll soon be able to play the music serviceably.

If you've been a practicing attorney for a few years – and done well through four year of college plus three of law school, then studied for and passed the bar – you already know many of the core skills of project management, especially project management in a legal environment. In fact, you've been managing projects as long as you've been leading cases.

You don't need to be Paganini on your first project; you just need to make it more successful than it would have been without your project management skills. Carnegie Hall is right across the street.

You are a fair viol.
William Shakespeare, *Pericles*

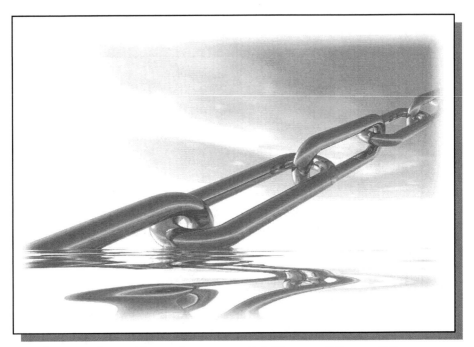

Tying the Basics to What You Know

The basic requirements of project management are straightforward.

You need to know where you're going. You need to know the steps most likely to get you there, how long they'll take, and what it will take to staff them. You need to know who has a stake in the outcome. You need to keep people informed about issues and progress. You need to know what's most likely to go wrong. And when you're done, you need to look back and learn from what went well... and what didn't go so well.

Most of these tasks correspond to work you do in the context of a case.

Know where you're going: You know the desired legal outcome when you lead a case: win at trial, file the patent, obtain favorable terms in the contract. What is the desired *project* outcome? Sometimes it's the same as the case outcome, but it usually includes additional factors: Not just file the patent, but do so by this *date* for a *cost* of $X. This step is part of the **project charter** (p. 158).

Steps to take: Each project is a series of tasks: Interview the inventor, research prior art, commission drawings, etc. Breaking a project into manageable tasks, and writing them down, is the key to staying on top of it.

Staffing the steps requires figuring out who in (or outside) your practice can handle each step at the right cost. Are they available when you need them? The cost-efficiency aspect may be new, but you spent much of law school figuring out how to divide up homework or Law Review articles. These two steps are called the **work-breakdown structure** (p. 192), often accompanied by a **budget worksheet** (p. 250).

How long the steps take is important to determining (or controlling) the cost of the project and to estimating a delivery date. This part may be new, but you probably have given estimates for your own tasks to others. Now you're the person who collects the estimates into **schedules** (p. 254) and considers the **dependencies** (p. 180) among the tasks.

Stakeholders include the broad variety of people who have a stake in the project. Sometimes, identifying the stakeholders is a project manager's most critical task. As an overt task this may be new, but you do it at least subconsciously when you negotiate something. You generally list stakeholders in the **project charter**.

Communicating is important but often forgotten in the heat of battle. Use LPM techniques to help organize and ensure effective communication, especially around uncomfortable topics.

What might go wrong is something attorneys already track, at least informally. A **risk worksheet** (p. 184) helps organize what you're doing.

Evaluating how the case went is likewise a task you already do.

To climb steep hills requires slow pace at first.
William Shakespeare, *Henry VIII*

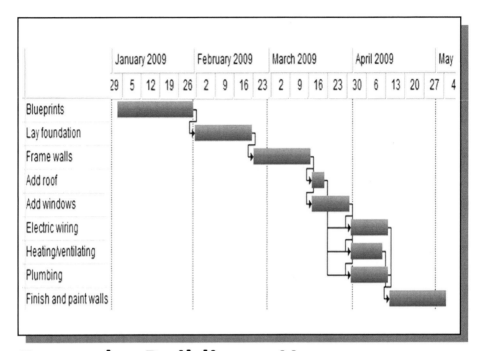

Example: Building a House

Let's take an admittedly very simplistic model of building a house to show how the pieces fit together.

A basic **project charter** (p. 158) includes a problem statement, what "Done" looks like, relevant deadlines, the client's budget, a list of stakeholders, and signoff.

You'd cover similar ground with the architect. The architect wants to know the problem statement, a/k/a why you want the house – vacation, retirement, for entertaining, etc. She'll ask what style you prefer, the approximate square footage, the number of bedrooms, and so on – the "Done" statement. Who's going to live there – just you, the kids, in-laws? They are stakeholders, along with any mortgage holder. Budget starts with what you're willing to spend (see below). The signoff is the agreement with the architect and perhaps the contractor.

A **budget worksheet** (p. 250) breaks out individual costs. Perhaps only the contractor cares about, say, foundation costs v. sheetrock expenses, but there are many elements that you yourself control, from lighting fixtures to roofing material to cabinets. The architect uses the budget and the "project charter" to inform the blueprints in the **Planning** stage (p. 168).

The general contractor creates a **work-breakdown structure** (p. 192) from the blueprints, determining how many hours of electrical work are required, how many person-days of carpentry, and so on.

The **schedule** (p. 254) lays out the various steps, as in the trivial version at left. Without a schedule, the general contractor can't line up plumbers and electricians. (Even with it, lining these folks up can seem impossibly hard; you'll likely see similar difficulties trying to line up busy specialists on a case.) The schedule also tells you when you can move in… though both house-building and project schedules often prove optimistic.

The contractor also tracks **dependencies** (p. 180). For example, the electrician can't begin wiring the house until the walls are up and the roof is on.

Communication is a contractor's best friend. The contractor will contact you regularly with progress reports. The architect will likely inspect the work every so often and let you know her views. Legal clients expect the same.

The contractor may not keep a formal **risk sheet** (p. 184) per se, but he has built contingency planning into both budget and schedule.

You **evaluate** the project afterwards starting with the acceptance walk-through, continuing with the housewarming party, and culminating in the inevitable vow to never do something like this again.

I do live in my house, and my house doth stand.
William Shakespeare, *Twelfth Night*

To Start, Keep It Simple!

There are a lot of moving parts in an all-up project-management effort.

My advice is to read through the spreads on Refining Technique (p. 124) and those within the four project stages: Initiation, Planning, Execution, and Evaluation. Gain an understanding of the concepts and the way the parts interact – but don't try to memorize all of it! Then, depending on the project, start putting the core concepts into practice, referring back to particular spreads for guidance on the appropriate approaches and techniques.

Suggested Items for the "Accidental" Project Manager

Start with the items and techniques with which you're already familiar:

- Write up a clear problem statement, phrased in terms of the client's *business* problem (p. 158).

- Add a "Done" statement describing a successful outcome (p. 154).

- Now add any relevant deadlines and the client's summary budget information. You've created the basics of a **project charter** (p. 158) that will serve you well.

- Add one more item to it, a list of the overt (obvious) stakeholders (p. 148), such as the client lead, the practice's client manager, and so on. Don't forget that you're a key stakeholder, too. Circulate the project charter to that list – email is fine for most projects – and ask for affirmative approval. Follow up until everyone agrees.

- Track **schedules** (p. 254), along with **dependencies** (p. 180) and intermediate deadlines if your case has them. You can do this in a spreadsheet, a word processor, or even on a whiteboard; you don't need a specialized tool at this stage.

To these, add at least rudimentary organized versions of a few things you've probably been tracking in your head, if not on "paper":

- Create a **work-breakdown structure** (p. 192) dividing the case into pieces no larger than ~40 hours. Then, in conjunction with your schedule, assign each of the tasks to someone, and get confirmation that they're on board with you. Remember that "work-breakdown structure" (WBS) is a fancy name for a list of tasks and who is assigned to them. As you gain project management skills, you may get a bit more sophisticated with the WBS; for now, don't get distracted or defocused by complex WBS or scheduling tools.

- List the clearest **risks** (p. 184) and your plans to avoid them.

- Create a detailed **budget worksheet** (p. 250) only if you can't get this information easily from your time-and-billing tool. You might omit this step for a matter handled entirely in house without chargebacks.

To show our simple skill, that is the true beginning.
William Shakespeare, *A Midsummer Night's Dream*

Doing What You Already Know

To climb
steep **HIILS**
requires SLOW PACE
at **FIRST**.

Brief #7

Checklist for Action

*If you're an experienced attorney thrust into a project management role
as an accidental project manager, pull together these items:*

✓ *Project charter consisting of a problem statement, a "Done"
statement, relevant deadlines, summary budget information, and a
list of obvious stakeholders.*

✓ *Get approval of the charter from the stakeholders listed in it.*

✓ *Project schedule, the simpler the better at this stage.*

✓ *List of dependencies on which scheduled items rely.*

✓ *Work-breakdown structure – tasks and who's assigned to them.*

✓ *List of risks and an outline of how you'll minimize them.*

Key Takeaways

- You are already doing more Legal Project Management than you realize.

- Start by working from what you know rather than trying to figure out all you don't know.

- The major items you need to track, plan, and organize aren't that complicated compared to the legal work itself:

  - Where you're going – the client's business problem and a brief summary of what it looks like when solved.

  - The steps most likely to get you to the solution.

  - How long those steps will take.

  - What you need to do to staff them.

  - What you plan to spend to do so.

  - The people with a stake in the outcome.

  - How you'll keep people informed about issues and progress.

  - What's most likely to go wrong.

- When the project is complete, look back and learn from what went well... and what didn't go so well.

Brief #8

Refining Technique

Groan and
SWEAT
under the BUSINESS,
either **LED** or **DRIVEN**.

What's an attorney's success rate at her first trial?

It has to be less than 50% on average. If verdicts have winners and losers, then there must be as many losers as winners. It's also logical that experienced attorneys will generally do better than novices.

Good trial attorneys keep refining their technique. They learn more, they make fewer missteps, they win more trials.

The same goes for project managers. Novices will make more mistakes than experienced project managers. However, remember that the experienced folks were themselves mistake-making novices at one time. And just as at trial, not all missteps are dispositive regarding the outcome.

But do all trials have clear winners and losers? Consider the vast number that settle ahead of the verdict; both sides are partial winners. Many trials result in a favorable verdict on one count but not on another; again, both sides are partial winners, where both attorneys helped their clients.

Project management is similar. Projects often have a range of acceptable outcomes, though, like trials, outcomes are scaled from highly favorable to acceptable.

Attorneys and project managers both start out as novices, often as apprentices in a sense. They learn, they make mistakes, they learn more.

The successful ones learn from both their mistakes and their successes. They analyze what they've done. They refine their techniques.

As a practicing attorney, you already have a number of project management techniques under your belt. Now it's time to refine them, hone them, and understand how to leverage them on behalf of your practice and your clients.

Call him to present trial. If he may find mercy in the law, 'tis his.
William Shakespeare, *Henry VIII*

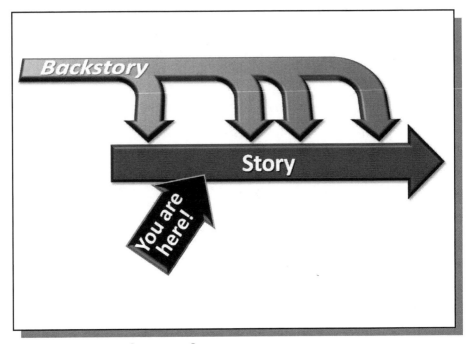

Story and Backstory

In a movie, the backstory is what has happened to the characters before the movie begins. It provides motivation for – the rationale behind – their actions. In the first *Star Wars* movie, for example, the key backstory was the tale of Darth Vader – why he wore that helmet, or, most famously, what the deal was between him and Luke Skywalker. That bit of backstory was never revealed in the movie; it wasn't until the sequel that we heard James Earl Jones intone, "I am your father."

Projects, too, have both story and backstory.

The Story

An early task when you take on a project is to understand its story. Who are the players? (See p. 148.) What do they want? Note that their wants may be in contradiction with their positions. What are their relationships with each other? What do they need from you to be successful in their jobs?

Equally important is how the project got to where it is today, whether you're taking it on at inception or *in medias res.*

The Backstory

The most critical information on a project is often the backstory, not the story itself. Only if you know the history can you fully able judge the impact of decisions and make sense of the varied inputs coming from the players. Only through the history can you truly plot the future.

All projects have backstories. How often, for example, does the project manager of a practice initiate a case? It does happen, but it's usually the client who puts the story in motion. The backstory includes what has happened to bring the client to your door.

Ferret out at least basic information about that backstory; it is essential to understanding the motives of the players and thus allowing you to satisfy the *real* client needs, not just the overt desires. The most successful project managers become investigative reporters on their own project.

The *Rashomon* Project

Rashomon is a famed Kurosawa film that tells a story from the viewpoints of four different people. Each one's story is complete, each story makes sense... and each utterly contradicts the others. When you join a project in progress, you'll encounter the Rashomon effect: each player has a different version of the events to date, a version that player fully believes. It's up to you to quietly develop a single backstory that represents the "one truth" as best you can discern it.

I long to hear the story.
William Shakespeare, *The Tempest*

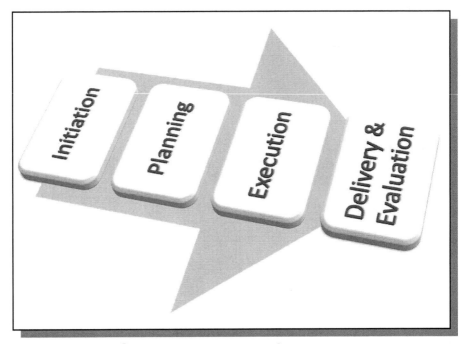

Stages of an LPM Project

All projects have the same up-front stages, though different types of projects have different endgames.

However, there are many different nomenclatures, and indeed different ways to apportion the work to specific stages. I want to focus on what works and what's easily understood, rather than on theory. I believe you can tell the project management story, at least for the Legal world, in a few hundred relatively short pages rather than needing thousands of densely packed sheets. Thus I use a scheme that is simple to remember and easy to understand.

The four stages here represent the lay of the land for Legal Project Management. The stages are slightly different from those of, say, an IT project. The largest variances are around post-execution steps; a technology project has long adoption/deployment and maintenance cycles, for example, that rarely apply to management of a legal case.

Let's consider an LPM project consisting, in brief, of four stages:

---

1. **Initiation.** Get the ducks in a row. Should we take this case? Is it one we can manage? For a firm, can we do so profitably? Let's say we take it. Who's the lead attorney? Who's managing the project, if not that attorney? Who are the key players? What do they need? Do we know what success – "Done" – looks like? If this stage is skipped – and it too often is given the most cursory attention – failure is predictable.

2. **Planning.** Who should work on the project? Are they available? What does the schedule look like? Does it fit within the deadlines? What are the big risks – and how can we mitigate them? What are our costs? For firms or departments that charge back, do we have agreement with the client on fees?

3. **Execution** centers on the actual legal work and generally consumes the vast majority of work time in Legal Project Management. (In other project management arenas, planning may be the longest stage.)

4. **Delivery and Evaluation.** What does the client get when we're done? (Most but not all legal projects have a small delivery stage.) What's the client's feedback? What's our own? What could we do better next time? Don't skip this stage no matter how rushed you are – especially the client-feedback part.

Process isn't the same as success, nor proceeding the same as succeeding. But by proceeding through these stages, you can control the case as a project rather than be controlled by its twists and surprises.

Afterward, determine our proceedings.
William Shakespeare, *Two Gentlemen of Verona*

Spiraling Into Control

You start on a project knowing little about it.

You know few of the details. You haven't yet discovered all the overt stakeholders, let alone the hidden ones (p. 152). There are risks and gaps you don't yet see (pp. 180, 184). There are the tradeoffs you will have to make (p. 170).

Your job is to move from the extremities of unknowing toward the center of knowledge. It's usually a spiral journey rather than a direct path, but you will get there.

Consider yourself a reporter researching a story you have yet to write. As with Legal Project Management itself, asking the reporter's questions about a project is the way you spiral into control of it.

Who, What, Where, Why, When, and How

The book's structure reflects the six questions reporters ask. The project manager asks those same questions:

Why is the client doing this project? Why is the practice doing it? (And sometimes... why have you been selected to lead it?)

What is the project *really* about?

Who are the players on a project, both on the project team and outside the team?

When are portions of the project needed? When can you deliver them?

Where (in what business/ legal environment) is the project happening?

How will you manage the business of the project (a/k/a project management)? And how will you do the legal work of the project?

"When" and "how" are Planning-stage questions. The rest are part of Initiation.

Joining a Project in Progress

You should still do the Initiation steps even if you are assigned as project manager to a case already underway. While some decisions will already have been made and plans laid out, you need to get a rapid handle on who wants what, who's promised what, how things are going, and so on – in other words, the six reporter's questions.

The hardest part about asking those questions on a story in progress is cordoning off the time to do so. The more chaotic the project environment, however, the more important those questions become. A bit of time researching them early on will pay off dramatically as the project unfolds.

Let all the number of the stars give light.
William Shakespeare, *Antony and Cleopatra*

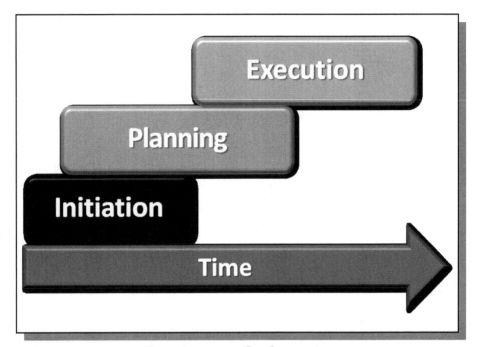

The Boundaries of the Stages

Professional project managers often talk about project stages as if they are immutable. However, to most people the stages seem to run together in real life.

How can you give a client an estimate during Initiation if you haven't yet done the requisite Planning? How can you even plan certain tasks if you haven't done sufficient Execution to get a practical ("heuristic") sense of how much work is really involved? Do project managers get some sort of special glasses, like the X-Ray Specs once advertised in comic books, allowing them to spot some ultraviolet delineator between one stage and another?

Well, as attorneys say... it depends.

Sometimes You Can Separate the Stages...

On many complex traditional projects, project managers will structure the project to force it into separate stages, with a "gate review" closing each stage to determine if the project will pass to the next stage. Thus they don't recognize the stages as much as define them, Humpty-Dumpty style. ("When I use a word... it means just what I choose it to mean, neither more nor less.")

Indeed, there are many types of projects where there is a natural order and progression. Each step is (relatively) orderly and self-contained.

However, legal projects done for paying clients rarely fall out so neatly, unless they represent repeatable work where you have deep institutional knowledge of the tasks. Clients want to know up front or early on what a case will cost, what you'll deliver, and when you'll deliver. Or worse, they'll *tell you* the answers they expect to all three of these questions. Yet as you'll see in Planning, these three variables – cost, scope, time – are interdependent, forming the resource triangle or iron triangle (p. 170).

...But They Often Flow Together

There's no reason on many Legal Project Management projects why Initiation and Planning cannot overlap. You might even model Initiation on some projects as a single point in time rather than a stage: "We already have the information to begin, so let's get onto Planning." For most projects, you probably do have this information; Initiation consists of collecting it, organizing it, and getting people to agree to its boundaries.

Overlap of Planning and Execution is more problematic; such an overlap would place you on the road before you know where you're going or how to get there. In the real world, not only does such overlap happen, but you must take it in stride and catch up while you're *on* the road (p. 201).

Some great exploit drives him beyond the bounds.
William Shakespeare, *Henry IV pt 1*

Business and Fiscal Literacy

Attorneys aren't, in general, trained in the fiscal matters of running a business any more than they have been trained in project management.

The latter situation is changing by necessity. The former must change, also, if attorneys are to help the practice by applying project management skills. Project management delivers work faster and more predictably while minimizing costs. Just as attorneys who understand practice profitability or a departmental cost center "P&L" (profit and loss report) will be better prepared to buy into LPM concepts, those who understand how costs are calculated will be better able to control them.

A Few Basic Concepts

Here are some key concepts legal project managers should understand:

Opportunity cost: A resource – an attorney, money, etc. – can do only one thing at a time. Money spent for project X is not available for project Y. Opportunity cost represents the work you cannot due because limited resources are applied elsewhere – in effect, the value of project Y.

Time value of money: Income expected, say, a year from now must be discounted when valued today – inflation, possibility of non-collection, opportunity cost, and so on.

Return on investment (ROI): What you get for what you spend, in terms of both total dollars (Euros, etc.) and percentage "profit." A later spread goes into further detail on ROI (p. 142).

Cash v. accrual accounting: Attorneys may not need to understand the intricate rules of GAAP (Generally Accepted Accounting Principles), but they do need to understand how the practice accounts for both one-time and recurring expenses. For example, partnerships using accrual accounting will handle staged payments on a fixed-fee matter somewhat differently from those operating on a cash basis.

Fully burdened costs are what a resource really costs the practice – salary plus overhead. Overhead includes everything from office space to health insurance, including non-billing employees in a firm.

Blended personnel costs: Practices sometimes don't share individual salary numbers. Instead, they provide an "average" cost for, say, a second-year associate.

Resource fungibility is a fancy term for the extent you can substitute one resource – e.g., an attorney – for another on a project.

RFPs (requests for proposal) are becoming more common, whether issued by an in-house department or received at a firm. See the spreads on p. 274 (for firms) and p. 308 (for clients) for more information.

Groan and sweat under the business, either led or driven.
William Shakespeare, *Julius Caesar*

Start Simply, Ramp Up

We're about to dive into the details of what goes on in project stages: stakeholder negotiations, communication strategies, resource allocation, return on investment calculations, and so on.

It's all part of Legal Project Management. (However, it is by no means *all* of project management, or of Legal Project Management; this book was even called <u>*Introducing* Legal Project Management</u> earlier in its life.)

Good project management is pragmatic project management.

Do only those things you believe will add value, will make a difference. If you do 50 similar H-1B immigration projects each year, you probably don't need separate budget workups for each. If you're already enmeshed in a case, don't chase after it with a belated ROI calculation for a decision already made. If the team has worked together before, you may not need to define the work process anew.

As you gain project management experience, you'll learn more about what works for you. You'll also encounter more varied situations calling for a broader range of techniques, and your increased experience will help you better understand their context and specific value.

Examples and Thought Experiments

The following examples are really thought experiments, not hard guidelines or even concrete suggestions. Use them to help you think about the complexity of the case and project you're facing. Consider which project management techniques might be most effective *for you* in situations such as these.

One-Attorney Project: For a project where you're the sole attorney, with or without paralegal or secretarial support, the list on p. 120 is a good set of items to begin with. Even some of those items might be overkill in a given situation, but there may never be a better time to learn about them.

Multiple Attorneys With Dependencies, Within One Practice: Add a schedule that captures dependencies (p. 186); step up risk tracking to a full risk worksheet (p. 184); and add an information radiator (p. 208). If the attorneys haven't worked together before, define a work process (p. 246) and agree on the way you'll make decisions regarding the case or its management (p. 244).

Complex Case With Multiple Practices or Third Parties: At this point, you're ready for the full-meal deal, all or most of the techniques and tools described in this book.

Complex Litigation, M&A, Electronic Discovery, etc.: These types of cases benefit from full-time Legal Project Management.

You have made a simple choice.
William Shakespeare, *Romeo and Juliet*

Refining Technique

Groan and
SWEAT
under the **BUSINESS,**
either **LED** or **DRIVEN.**

Brief #8

Checklist for Action

When you come on to a project, consider the following questions:

Initiation stage questions:

✓ **Why** are the client and practice doing this project/pursuing this case?

✓ **What** is the project (not just the case) about?

✓ **Who** are the players on and outside the project team?

✓ **Where** (in what environment) is the project happening?

Planning stage questions:

✓ **When** do you undertake the various tasks that make up the project? When can you deliver the result?

✓ **How** will you project-manage? How will you determine what you need to know and do, and what don't you know?

Key Takeaways

- Every project has both a story – what's going on – and a backstory – how it got here. You need to understand both.

- Different participants have different experiences of the backstory, different "truths."

- Legal Project Management projects have four stages:

  - Initiation

  - Planning

  - Execution

  - Delivery and Evaluation

- These stages often overlap in the real world, especially Initiation and Planning.

- Planning and Execution often overlap in practice, but this overlap can be problematic.

- When you join a project already underway, take time to do a mini-Initiation – at least privately – to understand story and backstory.

- Gain understanding and control of a new project, or one that's new to you, by asking the reporter's questions: Why, what, who, when, where, and how.

- Start with the Legal Project Management techniques you know, feel comfortable with, and/or believe add the most value to the current project. As you grow in your capabilities as a project manager, bring more techniques into play.

Brief #9

Project Stage 1:
Initiation

If
it were **DONE**
when 'tis DONE,
then 'twere **WELL**.

"I believe this nation should commit itself to achieving the goal, before this decade is out, of landing a man on the moon and returning him safely to the earth."

So said President John F. Kennedy in 1961. Was there ever a project with a clearer picture of success, of the goal, of "Done"?

During Initiation, you will create the three things that are most determinative, most dispositive of project success. First among equals is the "Done" statement. It tells you not just where you're going, but how you'll know you're there.

Second is the project charter, laying out the backdrop against which the project will play out. Who is the project for? What will it cost? Are there deadlines? And so on.

Third is the risk worksheet, trying to stay one step ahead of Murphy's Law. If anything can go wrong, it will... but we can try to prepare for it.

I've seen projects missing one, two, or all three of these components... but never a successful project missing them. They might be documents, they might be notes on a whiteboard, they might be sticky notes on the project manager's wall... but whatever the form, they must exist.

And the project manager must get the players to buy into all of them.

By the way, note the last clause in Kennedy's charge: "returning him safely to the earth." Maybe it's technically unnecessary – would America intentionally have sent someone to die on the moon? – but it serves as a reminder about the mindset needed on the project team. You can't focus just on the first 240,000 miles of the journey, the easier part. If you don't do the project entire, it's not done.

Myself the man in the moon do seem to be.
William Shakespeare, *A Midsummer Night's Dream*

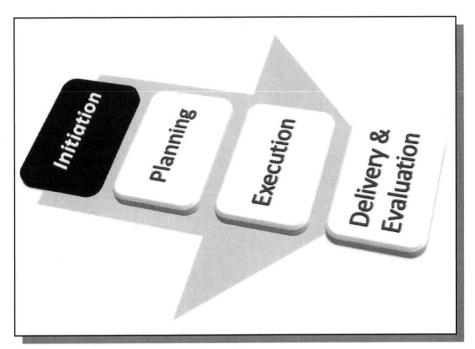

Overview: Initiation

In traditional project management, there is often a precursor to Initiation, an Evaluation stage leading to a decision on whether or not to do the project. While some legal projects may have such a stage, in most cases you'll gather Evaluation-type information during Initiation.

Use Initiation to drive out answers to four of the reporter's questions – which, though broken out in this spread, aren't cleanly divided into separate pieces in real life, or in real projects.

Why?

What problem is the client trying to solve? Clients have business problems, even if they're expressed in legal terms. A handful of items – Security and Exchange Commission filings, e.g. – may be cut and dried, but most involve business considerations. Fight a suit or settle? Business decision. Acquisition? Business decision. Make sure you understand the client's business need for which you'll provide legal services.

You or a financial controller will likely take a look at the practice's return on investment for taking on a project. What will it cost? What can you afford to spend? Don't shy away from this hard look at costs.

What?

What will you do to solve the client's business problem? What does success look like for you and for the client? Define "Done" along with a vision of the desired outcome. Remember that "Done" is not the same as perfect. The conditions of satisfaction (below) build on this data.

Who?

Identify the stakeholders within the practice and at the client. Note that some stakeholders may have competing interests; you need to discern these and build common ground. Not all stakeholders will be obvious, especially within the business client.

Define the project team. What types of resources do you need? Watch for specialists or one-of-a-kind experts you need to line up immediately.

Where (the Project Environment)?

"Where" refers to the environment in which the project/case lives: the client's world. For example, get clarity with regard to the client's expectations, especially if they are out of line with what you can do. Define the conditions of satisfaction for successful delivery, along with known intermediate or final deadlines.

Roll all the information gathered so far into a project charter.

Finally, estimate fees or chargebacks, and create a communications plan.

Let us take the law of our sides; let them begin.
William Shakespeare, *Romeo and Juliet*

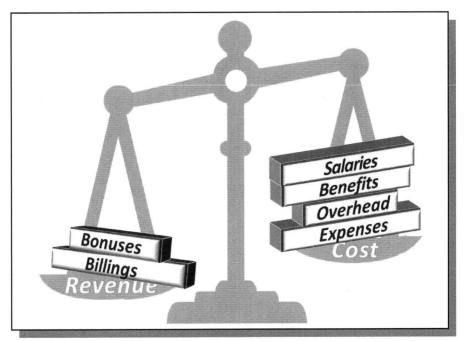

Costs and Return on Investment (ROI)

Calculating the ROI on a (non-contingency) case is far easier than defining it for a technology or construction project. The ROI calculator I use for evaluating legal-technology projects, for example, consists of 11 linked worksheets, hundreds of data points, and about 1000 calculations. The calculations for legal cases are generally much simpler.

ROI is basically *total* "profit," *or revenue minus total costs*, and profit *percentage* (technically, the internal rate of return), *revenue divided by total costs*. Since most cases are completed in less than a year or billed in phases, you needn't factor in the time value of money (e.g., inflation).

In-house ROI calculations are more complex: e.g., there's rarely revenue to the department, but there's often revenue to the client. I urge you to check out Cisco GC Mark Chandler's approach to evaluating which projects to do directly, hand off, or turn down (see the Bibliography).

Calculating Revenue for a Firm

Revenue is straightforward, with a potential complicating factor of a bonus for early completion or successful outcome. Assign bonus numbers a very conservative likelihood of attaining them. If there is a $10,000 early completion bonus and you believe you have a 50% chance of finishing in time, I'd halve the percentage – because things always go wrong – and add 25% x $10,000 = $2,500 to the revenue estimate.

Calculating Total Cost

The simple formula for cost is

Salaries + Benefits + Overhead + Expenses = Cost

Salaries can be specific to each person on the project, or blended – e.g., $X for paralegals, $Y for first-year associates, and so on.

Benefits – health insurance, e.g. – can be included in blended salaries, or you can get a percentage from your HR folks.

Overhead consists of two items: the per-person costs of phones, computers, rent, etc., and the apportioned costs of people who are not attached to projects, from the receptionist to an executive manager.

You can either wind up with lots of little numbers, or calculate an all-up cost per resource (person), either as a percentage of salary or included in a blended salary per level or position (secretary, second-year, etc.). The latter is easier to manage, and easier to keep consistent across the practice. Put HR to work helping you figure this out, if they haven't already done so (and if you have an HR department). If you need a number right now, use 50% of salary as a baseline.

Expenses are items neither charged to the client nor included in overhead. There are also risk expenses (see the next spread).

Avoid cost, and you encounter it.
William Shakespeare, *Much Ado About Nothing*

A Few ROI Subtleties to Consider

There are two other factors to think about in valuing a project. Remember, whether or not you're in a position to use ROI to evaluate taking on a project, it's still a project and practice goal to maximize value for both client and practice.

Opportunity Cost

Even if you make $1 profit, that's better than $0, so take any profitable endeavor, right?

Wrong.

Opportunity cost is the loss of whatever else you could do with the time and resources. If you take case X and then have to turn down the more profitable case Y – whether for lack of resources or because of an ethical conflict engendered by case X – you lose the value of case Y's opportunity. It's hard to calculate opportunity cost numerically; if you can't, let a senior partner or DGC make a back-of-the-envelope guesstimate. Remember, if you choose Door #1, you can't have what's behind Door #2.

There's also negative opportunity cost, the cost of *not* taking a case. If you decline to take case X and have attorneys sitting around who are neither generating revenue nor learning new skills, that's also rather costly. Look at the practice's overall prospects in considering opportunity costs.

Risk Expenses

Risk (see p. 184) is another factor worth considering. Imagine a case where you have a 50% chance of running $10,000 over budget. If you did ten such cases, you'd probably spend $50,000 more than expected, 10 cases x $10,000 x 50%. On each case, then, you'll spend *on average* $5,000 more than expected. That $5,000 should be applied to the cost side of the equation as a risk expense.

In calculating a risk worksheet via the method offered on p. 184, you'll also calculate risk expenses, the exposure *you* face on the project. Note that business exposure isn't quite the same as the concept of a client's legal exposure.

If the client bears some or all of the risk expenses, don't include in your ROI calculations the risk expenses charged to the client. For example, let's say you're billing hourly at $250/hour and have a 50% chance of needing to spend an extra 40 hours on the case. If the client agrees to cover the hours, you've transferred the exposure; it's no longer your risk expense. That said, there's still a client-satisfaction risk to charging more than expected – which is one of the reasons that you're employing Legal Project Management.

Most fair return!
William Shakespeare, *Hamlet*

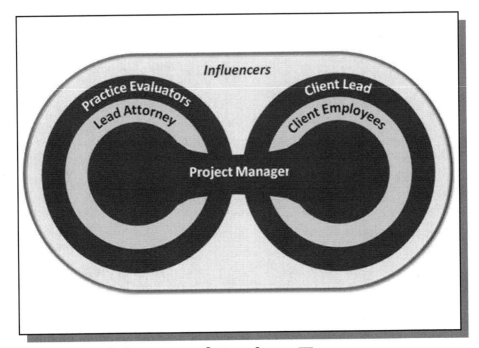

Stakeholders and Project Team

There are three groups of key players:

1. The stakeholders, detailed here.

2. The project team, also described here.

3. The influencers, described in the following spread.

Stakeholders

Some stakeholders for a legal project are those who have a business or career stake in the outcome, whether within the practice or in the client's business.

The Client Lead is the person with the business and legal problem that you're undertaking to address. The client lead should be a single person who is the final arbiter of your work.

The Evaluators will decide whether or not the project is a success. There are evaluators within the practice and at the client, including the client lead. At a firm, evaluators will likely include the client manager, a group of partners, and the Chief Financial Officer equivalent.

The Lead Attorney "owns" the case, charged by the client lead and the evaluators with its legal and business success.

The Project Manager, quite possibly the case's lead attorney, is responsible for the nuts-and-bolts planning and delivery of the case work.

Project Team

The Project Manager is both a stakeholder and the project team leader.

Legal Professionals include anyone in the practice working on the case – paralegals, knowledge management specialists, researchers, other attorneys, support staff, and so on.

Others: jury consultants, contacts at the client, bankers in an M&A deal, anyone whose work you need to schedule, track, and account for.

Needs, Wants, and Histories

Each stakeholder comes to the project not just with things they need but with a backstory, a history through which they view the work and your progress (p. 44). They also have interests (p. 152) – and it's to their interests that you can appeal to motivate them along particular lines. In few projects are the players truly aligned by default; good project managers just make it look that way.

I am tied to the stake.
William Shakespeare, *King Lear*

Assessing the Players

Influencing forces -- some obvious, some covert – can make or break not just the project, but the perception of its success, and of the project manager's success. The project manager must recognize, understand, and then influence the influencers.

It's unlikely someone in the practice will want to client to fail; that's a violation of professional ethics, for one thing. However, there may be those who would be happy if the project manager failed, or at least were adjudged to have failed.

Supporters make known their support of the project, though not always directly. Someone respected saying "cool case" carries a lot of weight.

Snipers attack the self-esteem and ego of the project team – "another dumb management idea" or "too bad they stuck you on that project."

Saboteurs actively work against project goals. They are more common on the client side or in-house as they play departmental politics.

Often common to both snipers and saboteurs is a worry that jobs are somehow threatened. It's up to you as project manager to change their attitude if possible; sometimes just hearing them out around decisions can go a long way. The other option is to neutralize them by inoculating the team, client lead, and evaluators against their opinions. Winning them over is best; moving them to neutral, no-comment status is okay; neutralizing their effects is a less effective choice; but letting them shoot at the project is high risk.

Kibitzers have low individual influence. Still, their sour-tinged comments affect how both the project team and those on the outside perceive the project.

Wait-and-Sees are influentials who visibly ignore the project. While a small number of wait-and-sees aren't a problem, the drag from half a dozen of them can be substantial. Understand their interests and tap into those interests to convert them to passive supporters if possible.

As project manager, identify – privately! – the members in each group. It's a fluid list. In the course of a project people will change camps. As long as they're moving away from non-support, change is good.

Client pressure for quality work at lower, more predictable cost is a good counter-agent for some of these players. However, recognize that others could be severely threatened by this pressure and by Legal Project Management in general. Someone who bills 2500 ineffective hours a year will go from being a hero in a billable-hours-based environment to low status in a performance-based firm. Likewise, an in-house attorney who works hard but fears responsibility may be exposed by LPM work.

Be alert in a firm for misalignment between the business client and her in-house attorney: different metrics, different budgets, different review goals. If you can't satisfy both, guide them in working through the issue.

You shall recount their particular duties afterwards.
William Shakespeare, *Much Ado About Nothing*

Stakes, Interests, and Positions

Fisher and Ury, in their seminal work *Getting to Yes*, observed that negotiations work better when the participants focus on their interests rather than their positions.

The classic example is two chefs who each claim the lone orange. They argue over it, and the best win-win they can come up with is to split it between them. However, if they'd worked from their *interests*, they'd have discovered that one sought the zest (rind), the other the juice.

Participants in a project, particularly stakeholders, rapidly stake out positions. Sometimes positions manifest in the form of "requirements," demands that the case include this or that. Sometimes they may appear to have little to do with what's at issue in the case, such as the position that only banker A or expert witness B will suffice.

Your job is to move the stakeholders gently from attaching to their positions to focusing on their interests.

The stake is the bedrock. It's career, money, reputation. Note that not all "stakeholders" actually have something real at stake; instead, they have interests and positions. However, they *feel* that they have something at stake, and must be treated as if they do. The big stakes belong to the client, the client lead, the evaluators at the client and the practice... and the project manager with career and reputation on the line.

Interests are what many "stakeholders" really possess. Understand what they believe will make their work-lives better – success in the case, advancement, recognition by management, a challenging project. You'll usually find it possible to devise a plan that can satisfy most or all of the interests (other than in some adversarial legal conflicts). The challenge is to build that plan with people clamoring about positions, and then convince them to trade rigid positions for achievable interests.

Positions are your potential downfall. They become atherosclerotic, hardening under pressure, blocking project flow. You'll be most effective in converting positions to interests in one-on-one discussions, where the position-holder isn't losing face by "backing down" in public. If positions harden in open discussion, change the topic or end the meeting. Transactional work in particular highlights the difference between interests and positions (see also p. 282).

The High Costs of Disparate Interests

Disparate interests can become expensive – expensive time, expensive people, expensive needs and wants. In adversarial matters, disparate interests and stakes are common – and even then, good negotiators can often help the parties find solutions that address most of their interests.

If it can be done under adversarial conditions, you can certainly do it on a project where everyone is putatively on the same team. Positions are almost always adversarial; it's up to you to convert them to interests.

What should that alphabetical position portend?
William Shakespeare, *Twelfth Night*

The "Done" Statement

What makes a good "Done" statement?

1. It is reasonably short.
2. It captures the essentials, the must-have focus of the project.
3. Everyone on the project can understand and buy into it.
4. If you reach "Done," the project will be a success.

A "Done" statement carries the goal of the project, not necessarily of the legal work at hand. For example, in a litigation matter, the goal of the legal work might be to win at trial or achieve a good settlement for the client. However, the project goal is to *manage* the litigation effectively and efficiently. In a trial, one side may win and the other lose – but both sides' projects can be managed successfully.

The project charter (next spread) must include "Done." While sometimes legal work must begin on no notice and with but a loose idea of the goal, the team must figure out "Done" as they get their arms around the case.

When a project feels like it's spinning out of control, pieces everywhere moving with the coordination of a herd of cats, "Done" is the lasso that pulls them back to a common center.

In Search of "Done"

Here are some questions that can help you home in on "Done":

Client: What does the client need? What does a successful conclusion to the matter look like to the client? Are there alternative good outcomes (settle instead of win at trial)? Are there budget or time constraints?

Practice: What does the practice need? Is that need aligned with the client need? If not, can you reconcile them (think interests, not positions – p. 152) or at least arrange them so they're not pulling in opposite directions? For example, DuPont works openly with its firms to train associates – at greatly reduced rates, which aligns interests and needs.

Players: Who needs to buy off on "Done"? Who may have a separate agenda? Does everyone understand that "Done" may not equal perfect, that budgets by default introduce limits and constraints?

The real world has limited resources, deadlines, budgets. If a matter is worth $10,000 to a client, and the attorneys run down every loose end to the tune of $20,000 worth of work, someone will be very unhappy. Either the client will overpay or the practice will eat the costs.

Practices are implementing Legal Project Management to avoid these situations. Keeping the focus on "Done" rather than on "do anything that seems useful" is the real-world response to real-world constraints.

If it were done *when 'tis done, then 'twere well.*
William Shakespeare, *Macbeth*

Expectations and Satisfaction

The client has certain expectations, even if she doesn't express them explicitly. Those expectations determine whether or not the client views the practice as successful in executing on a given case.

You need to take those expectations into account in structuring the case. Otherwise, you may miss the real target. You risk "winning" the case yet having a client who, seemingly inexplicably, is less than thrilled with your work.

Negotiating Expectations

Expectations should be part of the agreement between practice and client. In much legal work to date, the only shared expectation, other than standard ethical considerations, has been that the practice will work as hard as possible on the client's behalf. This has led to problems:

1. The client expects a particular legal outcome. Sometimes the practice tempers those expectations, such as explaining that juries can be unpredictable; too often, though, the client thinks the firm is working toward *outcome* and the firm is focused on delivering *quality* work – parallel, perhaps, but not the same thing at all. Mismatched expectations cause satisfaction issues and affect long-term relationships.

2. The client expects a certain level of value from the work. When there is no explicit agreement on price or scope, disagreement may linger in regard to the value of services rendered. Does the client want you to run down every potential loose thread, or does she want to spend only a certain amount? Again, mismatched expectations hurt.

3. The client expects a certain level of responsiveness, such as being "kept in the loop" or how fast – and at what hours – the attorneys return phone calls or reply to email.

Conditions of Satisfaction

The conditions of satisfaction are the criteria by which the client should measure the outcome of the project/case. The client will have criteria, whether or not she articulates them to you. It is your job, as project manager, to make those conditions of satisfaction explicit, usually in the form of the "Done" statement. In fact, in many professional-services organizations, the formal name for "Done" is conditions of satisfaction.

However, I recommend keeping a "service level agreement" (SLA) separate from "Done." The SLA covers responsiveness, billing frequency, status updates, and so on. It can and probably should be a standard agreement used across the practice. It may feel slightly distant and less collegial at first, but a good SLA, honored by client and practice, can enhance long-term relationships. Whenever you *beat* the SLA, you strengthen that relationship, building the business of the practice.

Oft expectation fails, and most oft there where most it promises.
William Shakespeare, *All's Well That Ends Well*

The Project Charter

A project charter is the most important project document you'll develop, keeping the project team focused on success. The project charter should be accessible by all stakeholders, team members, and influencers (within the limits of client confidentiality), although you may choose to create a "redacted" client version that doesn't show resources and budgets. An effective charter for an LPM project includes most of the following:

Client problem statement: What problem is the client trying to solve? Why has he called on you? State the *business* problem for which the client is seeking legal assistance.

Vision: Well-run projects generally offer a clear vision of the desired future state. In conjunction with "Done," the vision deflects distractions and scope creep. Test proposed actions against the vision to see if they align. Write visions in the present tense, representing the desired end-state. As the next spread explains, a vision isn't a "vision statement."

Done: What does success look like? How do you know you're there? The "Done" statement lists no more than two or three critical success factors (CSFs) for the project; if (when) you meet those CSFs, the project is successful.

Commander's intent, in the military, guides troop on-the-fly choices amid the chaos of the battlefield. Commander's intent is a worthwhile addition to the project charter whenever the practice itself has a goal for the project in addition to the client goal – e.g., train associates on some aspect of the case.

Out of scope: List the things you know that you explicitly will not do – such as the client instructing you not to settle before trial.

Any required dates or major deadlines belong in the charter. You don't need an entire judicial calendar in there, but if the case itself, say, hinges on a filing by a given date, put it in the charter.

Resources: Summarize the budget and resources available and committed to the project, whether by name or by position, e.g., "two associates." You can do a client-only version that omits this section.

Fees: What does the client expect to pay? Are there bonus payments? Any potential bonuses – outcome-based, early delivery, fees lower than estimated – should be noted in the charter as reminders to the team.

Key players: List as key players both the stakeholders and the leads on the project team.

Signatures: The stakeholders should sign off on the charter. It can be ceremonial for a major case, or a simple email – "Do we have this right?" – for the smaller ones.

Let me find a charter.
William Shakespeare, *Othello*

The Clear Vision

The vision represents the desired future state.

- "We have replaced the infringement on our client's patent with a license acceptable to the erstwhile infringer."

- "Our client has a new employee handbook that will both stand up to challenge and be understood and seen as equitable by the client's employees."

- "The client's records management process will meet e-discovery requirements while making it easier for the client to legally dispose of expired and unneeded records."

A vision is usually a bit simpler than "Done," higher level. Some project managers prefer to fold "Done" and the project vision into a single statement, basically by subsuming the vision into "Done." I'm all for simplification; however, the following story might offer a caveat.

The Power of a Vision

At Microsoft, one product team was determined to ship on time, facing the pressure of a very competitive market.

As they began development, the project managers (called program managers in "Micro-speak") created a one-sentence product vision and asked everyone on the team to sign it – literally.

At the start of each meeting to discuss features, one of the project managers read the vision aloud, even though that felt a bit hokey. Whenever someone brought up a new idea, the team would ask, "Does that fit the vision?" If it did, they discussed it; otherwise, they put it on the "wish list" for the following version and spent no more time on it.

The product shipped on time. There were no significant features that did not align with the vision set almost two years before.

Vision v. Vision Statement

Many corporations publish fancy vision statements, spending thousands of PR dollars to craft something that sounds good but is essentially meaningless. They come down to, "We make a profit selling good products," or "Don't be evil." (Oh, wait, that's a real one.)

A project vision needn't be polished; don't waste time playing wordsmith. It's not important – or efficient – to try to capture every nuance; in fact, getting too careful in creating a vision is what leads to those bland plaques cluttering corporate reception areas.

The vision serves as a reminder to the team; it doesn't replace the more detailed information gathered elsewhere.

Think of the clear vision as the label on a sieve through which you wish only relevant ideas to pass.

I have had a most rare vision.
William Shakespeare, *A Midsummer Night's Dream*

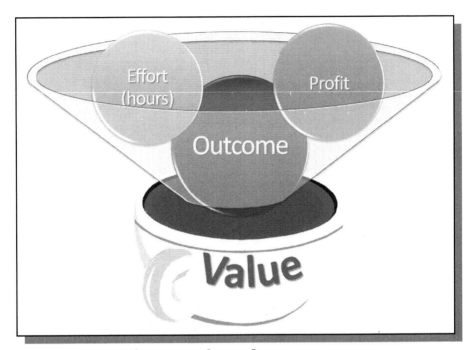

Fees or Chargebacks

Many attorneys dislike discussions of fees for three reasons:

1. They, like many of us, are uncomfortable discussing money, especially if it feels like putting a price on their self-worth (cf. the spread on communication on p. 164).

2. They feel slightly embarrassed by the high fees the firm charges. (They may also wonder about the mark-up on their own effort, often greater than 100%.)

3. They feel it somehow demeans the profession. Prices belong on soup and shoes; they violate the sanctity of a law firm.

In-house counsel are more comfortable discussing any chargeback costs with their clients; talking cost is taken for granted in the corporate environment. Oddly, these same in-house counsel don't always take the lead in the parallel discussion with their firms.

With Legal Project Management you are a participant in the business of your practice, as well as a legal professional. Especially in a firm, you're working to produce a profit for the business; if you're a partner or on the partner track, that profit becomes a big part of your income.

Fees are what the client pays for the value you deliver. You're delivering business value, and business value comes at a cost. If you can lower the cost for clients while providing the service they need at a good profit for the practice, you're on top of the game.

Cost v. Value

If you focus on cost alone, all three issues on the slide at left come into play. Take them out of play by turning the conversation to value rather than cost.

If a matter is worth $10,000 to a client, why should the client care – or know – how much work it takes to deliver that value? (Of course, that's speaking in the abstract, especially in a firm when clients are attorneys themselves.) When you buy something, you look at the value, at the quality for the price – not at how much it costs the company to produce and sell that good. While the client isn't buying soup or shoes, he is buying value, the value of your professional services. He's most emphatically not buying *effort;* "good try" doesn't cut it in the client's world.

The project manager may not be discussing fees or chargebacks directly with the client, though the client manager may ask you for an estimate before negotiating a client agreement. Either way, those fees and the discussions surrounding them directly affect both the structure of your project and the client's expectations; the better you understand them, the more effective you'll be in shaping and controlling the project.

What are thy due fees?
William Shakespeare, *Henry VI pt 3*

The Communications Plan

Initiation is the right time to build a project communications plan. For lengthy, complex projects such as a long trial or complex merger, I recommend a formal plan devised and shared with the project team. For many projects, creating a simple list will suffice, as long as you put recurring items on your (electronic) calendar.

Recognize that some discussions may be difficult or uncomfortable. Maintaining regular, open communications with the team and with the client will ease entry into these discussions, as will having an explicit agenda for such communications.

Make up a checklist as to how, when, and how often you will communicate about the following items:

Business problem: Make sure the project team and the client share the same understanding of the client's business problem. In discussing business issues with the client, focus on the long-term, strategic value of the relationship. If an in-house-attorney-client wants to discuss case strategy, set an agenda for the meeting to avoid drifting into micromanagement.

Discuss **conditions of satisfaction** (p. 157) and other elements of the **project charter** (p. 158) early with the client. In most cases, get the client's "written" approval (e.g., an email response) as an affirmative confirmation of what you've agreed on.

Scope (p. 172) represents the specific legal work to be done. Cover both the breadth and the depth of the practice's legal work for the client.

Be open and forthcoming about **fees and chargebacks** (p. 162). Start conversations with value, not cost. If you bill or charge back, plan how you'll discuss issues whenever you submit invoices or budget-transfer requests. Be proactive; don't drop the bill and wait for the client to call you. Coordinate any billing with periodic **status updates** to stakeholders in both client and practice management (p. 216).

Cover the **breadth/depth** tradeoffs (p. 173). Ensure the team is conversant with the **project budget** (p. 174); they can't stick to numbers they don't see and understand.

Determine how you plan to share **risk** data (p. 184) with the client and the team.

Determine with the team your **work processes** (p. 246), **meeting formats**/styles (p. 268), and **change management** steps (p. 210). Decide how you'll handle **decisions** (p. 244), and build a **responsibility matrix.**

Get started on an **information radiator** (p. 214) to collect the data discussed on this spread.

Alone she was, and did communicate to herself.
William Shakespeare, *All's Well That Ends Well*

Project Stage 1: Initiation

If
it were **DONE**
when 'tis **DONE,**
then 'twere **WELL.**

Brief #9

Checklist for Action

Communicate early and often about

✓   The business problem.

✓   The other elements of the project charter.

✓   Scope, including breadth v. depth of the legal work.

✓   Fees, chargebacks, project/case budget, and bills.

✓   Status updates.

✓   Risks.

✓   Work processes, meeting formats, and decision making.

✓   Change management.

Create an information radiator to collect and share this information.

Key Takeaways

- Initiation is about why, what, who, and where.

- Build the project around the client's business problem – which must be the first thing you identify and clarify.

- Understand the return on investment around the project/case for both the client and the practice.

- Use the ROI analysis to develop a cost structure and budget.

- Identify the stakeholders at both the practice and the client's business. Be alert for stakeholders who aren't in the foreground.

- Assess who can influence the project – for good and ill – at the client as well as within your practice.

- Focus on their interests and stakes; deflect discussion from their positions.

- Build a clear picture of the team you need for the project to be successful.

- What does "Done" look like? Above all, you, the team, and the client must agree on "Done."

- Determine the conditions of satisfaction for the project.

- Be clear with the client on the project's scope. Use "Done" and a clear vision to inoculate the project against scope creep.

- The project charter is the guiding document for the project; ensure all stakeholders agree and sign off on it.

- Don't be afraid to discuss fees or chargebacks up front with the client, but do discuss them in terms of value, not just cost.

- Fees and chargebacks are one item on the communications plan. Creating a communications plan up front takes an hour or two – and will save hours of pain, difficult discussions, and client unhappiness.

Brief #10

Project Stage 2: Planning

Nay,
PATIENCE –
or we **BREAK**
the sinews of our **PLOT**.

Dwight Eisenhower – the General who planned the D-Day landings at Normandy – once said, "Plans are useless...

"...but planning is essential."

Plans are useless, but planning is essential. Project managers can violate Ike's dictum in two ways. They skip the planning part, jumping right to execution, or they get so wedded to their plans that they adhere to them even when the world changes around them.

Sometimes, albeit rarely, jumping to execution works out. Not every project has risks that come to pass, dependencies that don't connect, clients with muddled needs. Still, risk #1 on any risk worksheet should be lack of project management; the more complex the case or project, the greater the exposure to that risk.

Occasionally, forcing execution back to the plan works out, too. Sometimes it only appears that the ground has shifted. More often, though, that approach presents the *illusion* of smooth operation: every overrun is explicable, every rough spot pounded down, every action superbly diagrammed by the unflappable project manager. But explaining overruns doesn't prevent them, nor is every action necessary or correct – and sometimes those rough spots are the complex nuances that spell the difference to the client between legal success and failure.

There is a broad middle ground inhabited by effective project managers, full of care about the project rather than full of themselves.

That middle ground is named Planning.

We? Fail? But screw your courage to the sticking-place and we'll not fail.
William Shakespeare, *Macbeth*

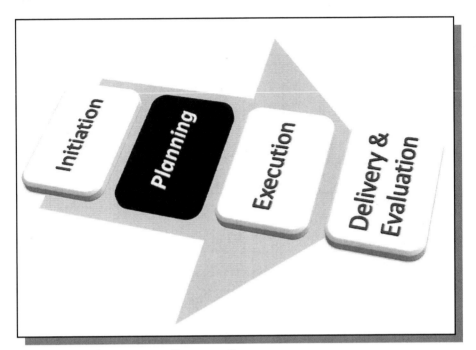

Overview: Planning

Planning is the heart of project management, legal or otherwise.

You don't *need* to plan; the smart people in your practice will get to the destination eventually, the way they always have. Planning helps the team find the most efficient route. Thus they participate in the profitability and success of the practice while delivering the most possible value to the client.

Much of the work in Planning centers on the resource triangle, the "iron triangle" (p. 172) that governs the tradeoffs among scope, schedule, and resources. You can't expand or contract one of these variables without altering at least one of the others – a relationship that's easy to see in theory but hard to remember under the pressure of clients pushing for more, faster, cheaper.

Planning also introduces resource allocation (p. 176) and budgeting (p. 174), creating a specific map for staffing the project – determining what levels of attorneys and others, identifying specific resources as much as possible, and setting out the budget for these resources. The goal is to deliver as much value to the client as you can within budget and available resources while also building the fiscal strength of the practice.

As you learn more about "resource" (people) availability and budget constraints, divide the project up into tasks of manageable size and complexity, called a work breakdown structure, or WBS (p. 192). While there are many highly formal approaches in project management to creating a WBS, I'll focus on a very pragmatic approach well suited to the legal world and Legal Project Management.

This is also the time to learn what you don't know, called gap analysis (p. 180). What don't you know about the legal issues? About the project itself? Start locating the factors that will affect the project schedule, especially dependencies (p. 182) and deadlines (p. 178).

Use this data to assemble a schedule (p. 190). The common "project management" software tools can be quite complex and hard to use without significant training or study. I'll talk about scheduling itself in this brief but will defer discussion of the tools themselves to p. 248.

What you *know*, what you know that you *don't* know, and what you *don't* know that you don't know add up to risk. Tracking and managing risk (p. 184) is the project manager's "safety net." You cannot avoid risk; rather, your job is to increase the likelihood of successful response to unplanned events.

Finally, beware of over-planning. For one thing, no battle plan survives contact with the enemy. For another, you can wind up in analysis paralysis (p. 196). Make the best decisions you can on the (partial) information available, and then adjust course as unanticipated events unfold.

Nay, patience – or we break the sinews of our plot.
William Shakespeare, *Twelfth Night*

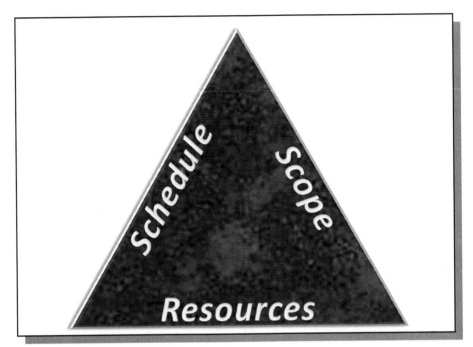

The "Iron Triangle"

The iron triangle, or resource triangle, is the key to effective Planning. (A triangle may not be a great metaphor, by the way, but it's a term all project managers use.) There are three major variables on any project:

1. **Schedule**: total number of days; "calendar time."

2. **Resources**, usually people, but resources can include any necessary item in limited supply.

3. **Scope**, the amount of work to be delivered, or project "size."

If you change the length of one element, you change *at least* one other element as well. For example, if I hold the scope steady but want to pull in the calendar, I need to add more resources, increasing the cost. Likewise, if I increase the amount of work (scope), I can either lengthen the calendar or add resources or both, which likewise increases cost.

Substituting Resources

The legal version of the iron triangle has a nuance that's usually minor in standard project management – the variety of resources available at different costs, from paralegal through senior partner. Some work can be done either by, say, an associate or a paralegal. The paralegal is less expensive but might require more supervision. On the other hand, the practice may benefit from the associate's on-the-job learning.

Using lower-cost but putatively less efficient resources is the one way in which a project manager can bend the iron triangle at least a little bit. If you're presenting estimates on a case (p. 258), consider two different levels of staffing, at least in what you share with the client manager.

Breadth, Depth, and Cost

The variable not shown on the iron triangle is cost. In the legal world, cost runs hand in hand with scope, subject to some resource substitution.

Scope, though, has two components: the breadth of ground to cover, and the depth to which you'll cover it. Increasing either breadth or depth adds cost and time. Thus it's important to get agreement up front with the client on scope, particularly scope depth. Few clients, when the question is put to them, are looking for exhaustive coverage on every aspect of the case. If the client wants to control cost, you can't run down every loose thread.

Calendar/Schedule Note

The triangle assumes that the resources are "maxed out," having no additional time in a day to spend on the project. You can sometimes pull in (shorten) schedules by shortchanging other projects people may be working on... or shortchanging family and personal time.

Both are expensive in the long term, leading to failures on other projects and the loss of good attorneys to burnout.

That's a threefold death.
William Shakespeare, *Henry VI pt 3*

Item	Internal Number	Cost/Hour	Estimated Hours Optimistic	Pessimistic	Weighted	Budget	Actual
Attorney1							
Attorney2							
Attorney3							
Attorney4							
Attorney5							
Attorney6							
Attorney7							
Paralegal1							
Paralegal2							
Secretary							
Other1							
Other2							
Other Expenses1							
Other Expenses2							
Travel and Entertainment							
Total Costs							

Budgets and Budgeting

Costs are what you spend to produce value, usually measured in money and/or time. Budgeting is how you manage and account for those costs.

Part of Initiation is defining at least a preliminary budget structure for the case. A budget structure or outline sets a total cost target.

As with costs, the budget can be based on money or time, with the former being more common. Personnel costs in the budget can be based on specific or blended costs and salaries (see p. 145); at Initiation and Planning, unless and until you know who will be working on the case, blended costs are a better marker.

The preliminary budget structure should be part of the project charter, though the charter need not show it in detail. If you share the charter with the client (generally a good idea) but don't want to share the budget details (also generally a good idea – talk about value, not cost), create or redact a client version of the charter.

The Project Budget Lifecycle

By the Planning stage, you should be fleshing out Initiation's budget structure. A structure lists the basic categories – personnel costs, expected expenses, and so on. Now is the time to add whatever data you have, such as expected hours or costs. It's okay to plug in default salaries + overhead if you don't have specific resources assigned yet.

On one shoulder sits a tiny experienced project manager yelling in your ear, "Don't budget yet. It's too early. You don't know enough." On the other shoulder sits an equally small client manager, yelling, "We need to give the client an estimate. Give me something to work with." In Initiation, you can plug in some very, very preliminary numbers as targets. However, I strongly recommend that you wait until Planning is well underway to incorporate detailed numbers.

There are exceptions. It's reasonable that if you have amassed data on a specific, repeatable type of case, such as drafting a patent, you should have a pretty good idea of the budget on other such cases... and the client will have the same expectation around the fee.

On the other hand, you often hit Planning with fee negotiations having outraced project progress, or where the client manager has already suggested a fee. In this rather common case, the project manager must find or negotiate the balance between "Done" and profitability, often by triangulating in on the conditions of satisfaction; see p. 260.

The Space Shuttle

Clients sometimes ask for the sun, the moon, the stars, and the space shuttle, because they don't recognize the cost. You have an obligation – some would say a fiduciary duty – to help the client understand the costs of a request. Perhaps a Titan rocket would work well enough....

Many times I brought in my accounts, laid them before you.
William Shakespeare, *Timon of Athens*

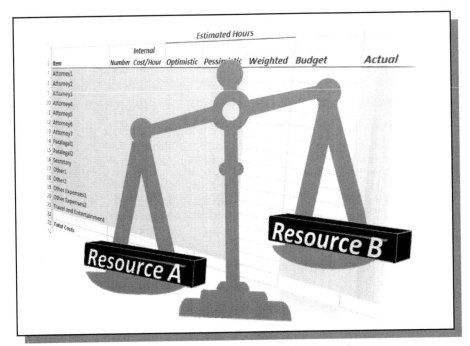

Resource (People) Allocation

Who will do what on the case? How do you get the right resources at the right time... and right cost? "Resource" is a project management term often synonymous with person, but resources are anything in limited supply, other than time itself – people, conference rooms, IT work, etc.

You'll usually unearth the details during the Planning stage, even if during Initiation you started lining up the people you knew you'd need, confirming availability. In practices where attorneys have some say in what they work on, it doesn't hurt to whet their interest in the project as early as possible.

As part of budgeting for resources, get your mental engine working on various tradeoffs, assuming you're not the only attorney on the project. For example, consider this tradeoff between two attorneys with requisite skills, knowledge, and availability:

- Attorney P is a senior partner. Her internal cost is $700/hour fully burdened (including benefits and overhead). She bills out at $1000/hour, but you're not going the hourly route on this case.

- Attorney Q a fifth year, probably partner track. His internal hourly cost is $350.

All other things being equal, attorney Q is the more cost-effective project resource. However, all other things are never equal. Consider:

- Attorney P, because of her experience, is likely to be more than twice as productive (effective work per hour) given the complexities of this particular case. Thus her cost per unit of work delivered is actually lower than Attorney Q.

- While both attorneys have time available, Attorney P's experience makes her more valuable to *other* projects, and she's doing more and more rainmaking. For the practice as a whole, it might be better to utilize Attorney Q on this project.

- As a project manager, you're slightly intimidated by the prospect of directing the work of senior partner P. Should you do what's easier… or take on a challenge to build your own strengths?

Thinking through the tradeoffs in resources also helps you think about different ways of approaching the work on the case. Note that there's no cut-and-dried answer in the example – hence the term "tradeoffs."

The Critical-Path Resource

What if there's but a single practice specialist with the knowledge and skills needed for the case, or a facet of it? You need to negotiate with others in the practice – and the specialist herself – for her services sooner rather than later. Ideally, the practice shouldn't commit to the project until you're confident you have the skills to staff it.

She cries, "Budget!"
William Shakespeare, *The Merry Wives of Windsor*

Deadlines

One place attorneys come to Legal Project Management with a bit of an advantage is their familiarity with the way deadlines affect the flow of work.

Judges expect attorneys to make their court appearances. It takes a Katrina-sized hurricane to excuse missed filing dates. Attorneys write deadlines *into* contracts as well as deliver contracts *by* deadlines. Almost every branch of law has deadlines almost as implacable as the original "dead line" (at the Andersonville prison during the American Civil War, a line of posts beyond which the guards would shoot a prisoner).

When is the client expecting various work items from you? When can you deliver them? What are you telling the client about delivery dates? What other deadlines are in play, such as court dates or Rule 26 meet-and-confer sessions? All of these types of deadlines should be tracked as part of Legal Project Management – court-imposed, client-imposed, third-party, internal promises, and the like.

Deadlines and Dependencies

A dependency in Legal Project Management (pp. 182, 250) exists when one task or deadline depends on another. If you're depending on someone or something else that misses a deadline, you have but a handful of options: do your work in less time, do less work, extend the deadline, or get more help. At the Initiation stage, you were largely gathering up all the deadlines and dependencies you know about; in Planning, you now look in detail at how these deadlines and dependencies interact. You also need to spot hidden dependencies, both those not called out and "transitive" dependences where A depends on B which depends on C.

Negotiating Deadlines

Not all deadlines are fixed in stone; even some court dates yield to continuances. Most importantly, do not accept client deadlines as unyielding without at least testing the proposition. External events drive some client deadlines; many are driven by the client's own internal wants and needs; and some are pulled from thin air. That said, deadlines do concentrate the mind, as Samuel Johnson noted about the prospect of being hanged in the morning.

Try not to commit during Initiation to client internal deadlines; use your Planning work to reveal whether or not you can meet those deadlines with sanity and safety. While you can bully someone into committing to an unreachable deadline, you can't bully them into meeting it.

Deadlines and Schedules

Scheduling is the allocation of resources against those deadlines. Actual resource allocation is usually part of the Planning stage. An initial discussion of scheduling begins on p. 186.

They are recorded in this schedule here.
William Shakespeare, *Love's Labors Lost*

Gap Analyses

Examine three gaps in planning a Legal Project Management project:

1. **Legal:** What is the gap between the client's current situation and the desired legal outcome?

2. **Project:** What's the gap between what you do know about the project and what you *need* to know, have, and do to succeed?

3. **You:** What's the gap between your skills as a legal project manager and what you need to learn vis-à-vis this case?

The Legal Gap

The core work of an attorney has always been to close the first gap; attorneys are skilled at identifying and addressing the client's issues.

Legal Project Management's main bridge over this gap is the focus on solving the client's business as well as legal issues; solve the former as well as the latter to build strong, long-term client relationships.

The Project Gap

Legal Project Management helps you identify and close the gaps in the project itself. Be on the lookout for these types of issues in particular:

* **Resources** that you haven't named, haven't located, or who may be unavailable.

* **"Done"**: Lack of agreement on the two or three things you absolutely must attain to call both the project and the case a success.

* **Dependencies**: Can you trace the connections between all of the things you need to do plus the things and people you need to rely on?

* **Financial**: Does the team understand the client's budget?

* **Open (undecided) items**: What hasn't been decided that you must clarify? What open items could cause a shift in the project or case?

* **Misaligned assumptions**: Cross-check all project assumptions with the various players – just as you already do with legal matters.

* **Work process and decision-making**: Is the team agreed on how work will be passed off between members, how legal and project decisions will be made, and how you'll resolve conflicts?

Each of these gaps, whether canyon or lacuna, represents a risk to the project. You need to mitigate these risks and build contingency plans for those you cannot completely erase (p. 184).

Your Own Gaps as Project Manager

Consider what you know and don't know. Use this book as a refresher and guide. The hard part: things you don't know that you don't know!

How soon confusion may enter 'twixt the gap.
William Shakespeare, *Coriolanus*

Dependencies

"For want of a nail...." Schedule dependencies, resource dependencies, other-party dependencies, work-product dependencies – either you manage them proactively or you incur a high risk of failure.

When one task or deadline depends on another, a dependency is created. For example, if you live in Westport CT and want to be at your Manhattan desk at 8:30 AM, you could have a dependency on the 6:50 AM train. For now, I'll limit the discussion to the most common type of dependency – you cannot begin task B until task A is complete. This is called a finish-to-start relationship, described further on p. 186.

In Initiation, you identified all of the dependencies that you could, tracking them in your risk worksheet, on a project plan, on index cards.... Now, in Planning, you'll build a richer list and learn more about each dependency – and plan how to manage it.

Schedule (Event) Dependencies

Schedule dependencies are common, where one event depends on another. Many such dependencies are commonplace; for example, you can't move forward with a patent infringement trial until the Markman hearing. However, some events, especially those out of your hands, can wreak havoc with a project if you don't recognize and manage them up front. For example, you send a contract to the other party and allow four days for its review; what happens if they don't get to it? If they have questions? If their counsel questions terms you thought were settled?

Resource Dependencies

If you can use resource A or resource B interchangeably, they are said to be "fungible" – proof that economists love Latin as much as lawyers. In Planning, focus in particular on the non-fungible resources. Is there only one bankruptcy specialist in the practice? Do you need a particular expert witness? Is your e-discovery system ready to handle this case?

These dependencies represent risks you need to mitigate as soon as possible. What's the cost of a retainer for the expert you might need compared to the cost of not being able to use him... or of his working for the other side? Track these dependencies as you spot them, a process that will continue at least through Planning and usually into Execution.

Other Dependencies

Are you relying on another attorney's work product? The client supplying certain documents? Other parties doing something? Each is a risk to the project, whether to its outcome or its schedule.

Not all dependencies are a house of cards. All projects are chock-a-block with dependencies. Successful project managers track and manage them early – before they end up managing you.

Tell me whereon the likelihood depends.
William Shakespeare, *As You Like It*

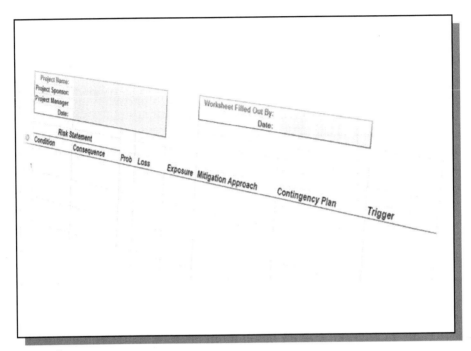

Risk Management

Legal Project Management helps you achieve success with both planned and unplanned events.

It's easy to focus on the planned events, but effective project management is least of all about organizing schedules, which consist of planned events. Your ability to recognize the possibility of unplanned events – risks – and either mitigate them proactively or react effectively determines your success. A **risk** is any event, planned or unplanned, real or potential, that would noticeably affect your project.

Nothing derails a project faster than encountering an unexpected, unmitigated risk. The easiest way to add a meaningful touch of project management is to track potential risks, with mitigation and contingency plans: no cost, little pain, and significant gain. See p. 186 for the six factors you should track for each risk condition.

In Legal Project Management, you'll generally ignore risks at the extremes: the minimal – someone's out sick for a day – and the catastrophic – Hurricane Katrina. The former cost more to track than you could ever save by chasing them, and the latter have neither mitigation nor effective contingencies beyond the practice's overall business-continuity planning.

Keep track of how risks change over time. On most legal projects, weekly risk analysis will work well. Don't try to identify all the risks yourself; ask the project team and the stakeholders for their insights. Share the risk worksheet across the project team. Also share it from time to time with the stakeholders as a summary when you update them on progress.

Risk management, with its attendant tools, isn't limited to project risk. Consider using the same method to systematically manage case risks.

Each time you review your risk data, keep an eye out for any risks added since the last review. Also watch for any risks where the probability or exposure has changed. It's good to know which risks are fading as well as those moving toward the top of the charts.

Track risks until their probability reaches 0%, meaning it can't happen or its window has closed, or 100%, meaning the trigger event has occurred and you're now running the contingency plan. You might take a weekly snapshot of the risk worksheet to help spot trends and changes. Those snapshots also let you better understand the way risks change over time, knowledge you can apply to subsequent projects.

The Attorney as Risk Manager Rather Than Gatekeeper

Clients are asking attorneys to be legal risk managers, *mitigating* risk rather than acting as naysayers or gatekeepers to reduce risk to 0%. It's the business owner, the client, who must own the risk, deciding an acceptable level of risk based on the attorney's advice. Attorneys must learn to document their approaches to risk and their analyses of risk – and document also that the business is willing to take a given risk.

> *All great fears, which now import their dangers, would then be nothing.*
> William Shakespeare, *Antony and Cleopatra*

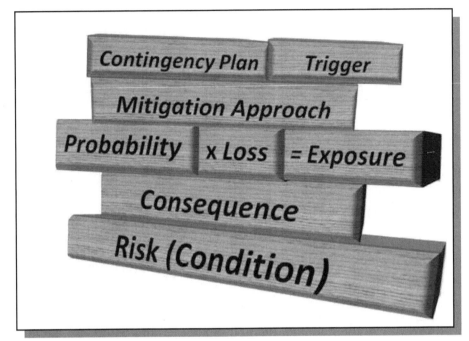

Risk Worksheet

Perhaps the most important – and least used – document in project management is a risk worksheet. At some level, everything on a project could be managed by anticipating, understanding, and mitigating or avoiding the risks.

It never fails to astound me when I come onto a project and discover that there is no systematic risk tracking, whether in a spreadsheet (probably the easiest tool), a document, a database, or even a wall chart.

Many project management all-up solutions (p. 248) contain a tool for tracking risks. On the other hand, a spreadsheet also works well and likely doesn't require you to learn anything new. Shared online spreadsheets such as Google Docs offer some interesting advantages, but if you have security or confidentiality concerns, Excel and other desktop spreadsheets work quite well also.

The Risk itself is the starting point, the condition that could threaten the project if it comes to pass. There are six factors to track for each named risk, plus a time dimension (how risks change from week to week):

Consequence: What happens if the risk comes to pass? Is it a delay, additional cost, project failure, egg on your face, extra pressure? Stating the consequence in words helps the team focus.

Probability is the likelihood, as you understand it at present, that the condition (risk) will occur. This needn't be some exact number; "T-shirt sizing" precision is sufficient (small, medium, large, extra large). Express it as a percentage, and keep your eye on it until the probability goes to 0%, meaning the risk is gone, or 100%, indicating the condition has happened. Here is where the time dimension is most helpful. Is the probability increasing or decreasing? How worried should you be?

Expected Loss is the cost to the practice and/or the project if the condition occurs. If you express it as a monetary value, it will be easy to size risks against each other and determine your **exposure**, the probability times the expected loss. Sort the risks by exposure each week to get a sense of the project's biggest danger zones.

Mitigation Approach: What can the project team to do minimize either the likelihood of the risk, the expected loss, or both? There may be multiple mitigation opportunities. Some project managers keep a risk log to track mitigation steps taken and the changes wrought thereby.

Contingency Plan: Mitigations minimize risk *before* it occurs; contingency plans are kicked off when the condition comes to pass, in order to minimize the damage to the project. Some risks may not have (useful) contingency plans, such as a client shutting a project down.

Trigger: The team needs a clear signal that a risk condition has occurred, that it's time to put the contingency plan into action.

Danger dogs the heels of worth.
William Shakespeare, *All's Well That Ends Well*

Risk Worksheet

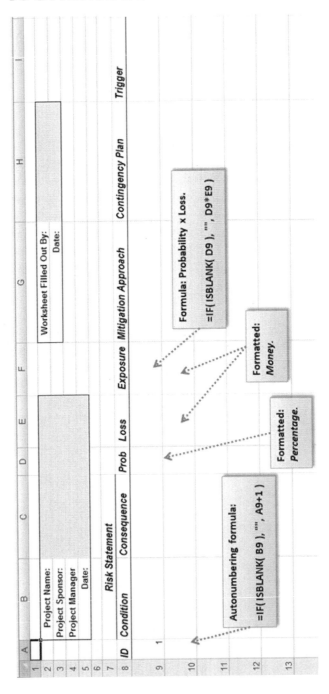

Risk Worksheet Example

Project Name:	Legal Project Management			Worksheet Filled Out By:	Steven Levy
Project Sponsor:	Anya Smith			Date:	September 30, 2009
Project Manager:	Steven Levy				
Date:	August 14, 2009				

Risk Statement

ID	Condition	Consequence	Prob	Loss	Exposure	Mitigation Approach	Contingency Plan	Trigger
1	Sponsorship lost	Program canceled	10%	$200,000	$20,000	Keep sponsor informed; stop by regularly (5 mins) to touch base	N/A	Message from Sponsor or Exec Manager
2	Poor attorney attendance at training	Poor LPM uptake, program probably seen as failing	30%	$150,000	$45,000	Sponsor helps get partner to commit attorney time. Follow regularly to ensure attorneys are on board. Reminder mails boosting program at T-8 and T-2 days.	Asked trainer to have ready 30 mins preparatory but non-mandatory exercises if attendance is low at start. Sponsor agrees to call missing participants if >10 mins late. Announce/provide quality breakfast and lunch.	Less than 65% attendance 10 minutes after scheduled start time
3	Poor alignment or timing between initial cases available, training start, and attorneys signed up for training	Considerably harder to get the program rolling because of gap between learning and practice	30%	$50,000	$15,000	Review with sponsor of new-case intake at T-8 days to assign cases. Sponsor has sent mail to client managers apprising them of program; awaiting responses.	Trainer will remain onsite for second day -- scheduled as proactive coaching but convertible to makeup training. (Should we also use this to mitigate low attendance?)	Fewer than 65% of scheduled attorneys have appropriate cases in hand at T-1 days.
4	Training day canceled for snow or other office disruption	Minimal if one-day delay, though some attorneys may not be able to make the makeup day	10%	$5,000	$500		Convert first coaching day to training; add additional coaching day as soon as training group can make right person available.	Office closed or majority of attorneys out for some reason

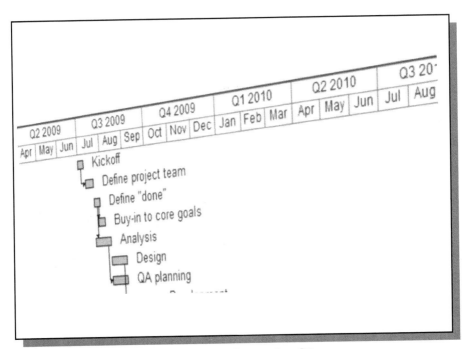

Schedules and Scheduling

Scheduling is the most visible piece of project management, especially to those starting out. Open a software program such as Microsoft Project, and you're confronted immediately with a blank "scheduling" form.

Scheduling, though, is rarely as important as the people-herding, budgeting, risk-management, and decision-making aspects of Legal Project Management. The more detailed the project schedule, the harder it is to maintain, and the less people will attend to it.

In addition, the legal world is beset with externally enforced schedules into whose deadlines you must fit – court calendars, filing dates, meetings with clients and third parties, and so on.

Scheduling is the art of arranging tasks in logical order to meet your deadlines.

Representing Schedules Visually

Project schedules are often shown as Gantt charts, a linkage of tasks, dates, and dependencies (see the slide for a fictitious example). Gantt charts are instantly recognized by project managers, but they are hard to set up properly without significant practice or training (see p. 260).

Many project managers track tasks in spreadsheets. That provides a simple, even simplistic view, but it's a view that is easy to understand and maintain.

Finally, most practices with significant court calendars use specialized software to track those calendars. Sometimes you can import or link this data with a project scheduling tool, or the tool itself provides a way for you to add non-court dates and tasks. Keeping information in two places is a recipe for one of them being out of date. Murphy's Law says someone will rely on the out-of-date, incorrect version for critical information.

Scheduling is detailed as part of Practical Legal Project Management (p. 254 ff.).

The Most Important Factors in Scheduling

The most critical need is a viable work breakdown structure (WBS), a fancy term for a list of the project's tasks and the person(s) assigned to them. (A formal WBS also shows the hierarchy among tasks.) The key to a good WBS is keeping tasks of a reasonable length – not so short that they become painful to keep track of and you wind up leaving things out, but not so long that they lose key details – i.e., 8 to 40 hours.

In terms of what tasks depend on what, focus on those leading most directly to "Done," and those on which "Done" has the most dependencies. A later spread delves further into dependencies (p. 250).

Finally, if you set up the chain of dependencies correctly – and this is very hard to do – you can use a scheduler to calculate schedules (p. 254).

I will give out diverse schedules.
William Shakespeare, *Twelfth Night*

	A	B	C	D	E	F	G	H	I	J	K	L	M
1								Hrs					
2				Task	Total	Secr.	Para	Assoc 1	Assoc 2	Atty 1	Atty 2	Sr Atty	Internal Cost
3	2.			Review contract									
4	2.	1.		Send for revision									
5	2.	1.	1.	Internal review/scrub	17	1	4	2	6	2	2		$1,878
6	2.	1.	2.	Send/track copies	8	6		2					$421
7	2.	2.		Review changes									
8	2.	2.	1.	Indiv. change reviews	27	3	6	3	3	5	5	2	$3,509
9	2.	2.	2.	Collate changes and comments	11	8	2			1			$558
10	2.	2.	3.	Conference review	15	3	2	2	2	2	2	2	$1,965

The Work-Breakdown Structure

A formal work-breakdown structure (WBS) is like a detailed outline of the project, complete with outline-style numbering (e.g., "2.1.4"). That level of formality may be overkill for attorneys simply trying to manage large legal projects, but core WBS concepts are easy and important:

- **Completeness**: All work is included in the WBS. If it's not in there, it's not (currently) in the project. Include your own tasks, too.

- **Uniqueness**: No single piece of work appears in more than one item.

- **Outcomes**: Items are deliverables, not methods; "what," not "how."

- **Five Days**: Create items of manageable size, e.g., one to five days.

- **Resourced**: All work on each item is assigned to one or more "named resources," whether real ("S Levy") or generic ("Associate 2") names.

Although you may choose to skip the outline structure, it's still helpful to organize items by scope – e.g., you might break a litigation WBS into pre-service, pleadings, discovery, interrogatories, and so on.

Details and Dependencies

Clearly, it's a lot easier to get down to the requisite level of detail in, say, a patent prosecution than litigation; each such case may take a year or more, but the former is both repeatable at the detail level and much less subject to unpredictable variability induced by other parties. Classify as much as you can, when you can; for the rest, use a SWAG, a Sophisticated Wild-A** Guess. Label these items SWAGs; the 40-hour rule doesn't apply until you understand more and can transform a SWAG into estimates.

As you learn more, update the WBS with better estimates (p. 250), breaking apart longer tasks that are no longer SWAGs.

Most WBS items have dependencies, other items that must be completed or at least started (p. 250) before you can begin (or finish) the given item. If you're using a project management tool to create the WBS, you can easily attach dependencies. If you're using a spreadsheet or even Word table for your WBS, record dependencies as text in a separate column.

Don't overcomplicate the WBS; it's just an upwardly mobile task list.

Resources and Budgeting/Costs

You can start with a "visual" WBS (see the slide) and then later transform it to a list with resources. One of the side benefits of assigning resources to WBS items is that you can quickly build a project budget, especially when using project management software or spreadsheets.

The completeness and uniqueness requirements do double duty as they ensure that each work item is counted exactly once in the budget.

Breaking down the pales and forts of reason.
William Shakespeare, *Hamlet*

Short- and Long-Term Planning

There's a corollary – actually a predecessor – to Eisenhower's dictum that "plans are useless, but planning is essential." Nineteenth century military theoretician Helmuth von Moltke noted that "no battle plan survives contact with the enemy."

Strategy and Tactics

Commander's intent (p. 158) is also a von Moltke concept. Throughout a case attorneys will have to make decisions on the fly, in situations that don't match those of planning sessions. Such situations are highly visible in court or during negotiations, but even a first-year associate researching cases and precedents must choose which of them he will carry upstairs to the senior attorney seeking them.

Attorneys start work on a case by defining or clarifying the goal and them designing a **strategy** they believe will achieve the goal. That strategy then governs the specific initiatives and actions – **tactics** – the case team will use.

However, tactics often break down or come up short under execution pressure; if the people working on the case don't understand the lead attorney's commander's intent – goal and top-level strategy – they will have to either guess or wait for instructions, neither of which is efficient.

Expecting the Unexpected

You manage the "business" of the case – Legal Project Management – the same way: You have a goal and strategy to achieve it. Then something unexpected happens. Thinking as an attorney, you wouldn't react blindly; you'd consider how to turn it to your advantage, bearing in mind your (the client's) goal. ("Did they just reveal a bombshell... or a distraction?") Likewise, thinking as a project manager, don't react blindly to the unexpected or fret that it doesn't map to your project plan.

On projects, expect the unexpected.

The successful project manager views the unexpected event in terms of the project's goals and strategy. You may or may not be able to turn it to your advantage, but you must deal with it in a strategic context, in how it fits into "Done." Map it not to the plan, but to the goal.

Project Stages v. Legal-Case Stages

By the way, consider that *project* Planning may not coincide with legal-case Planning. Planning for trial, for example, is actually part of the Execution stage of a litigation Legal Project Management project, and for large cases may well constitute a project in itself. Usually, project Initiation and Planning will run ahead of the similarly named case stages.

Thus directed, we will follow in the main battle.
William Shakespeare, *Richard III*

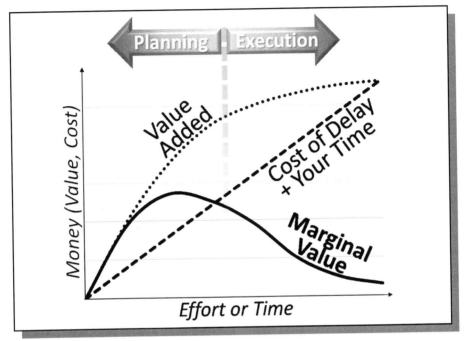

Analysis Paralysis

During Planning, the more you study and analyze, the more you'll learn. You can more accurately define tasks, build crisper schedules, gather a broader set of risks.

And you can eat away at the total time available for the project.

Going to Extremes

The danger during Planning comes from the extremes. The danger posed by too little time spent in Planning is obvious, but there is also danger from too much, a situation known as analysis paralysis. Extending Planning beyond a reasonable point is not an efficient use of time or budget; the value such additional planning adds is less than the cost to do the added work.

All project managers are forced to make decisions from partial information, just as attorneys are. In the past, attorneys have sometimes had the luxury of almost unlimited paid time to delve exhaustively into a matter. There are occasional matters of such import – "bet the business" choices – that call for the ultimate in depth, but clients are increasingly unhappy about the value they receive when they don't ask for such depth... but receive it – and have to pay for it -- anyway.

It's the project team that will pay for analysis paralysis. Work gets pushed up against deadlines because the team is waiting on the project manager for decisions. The client eventually pays, too, because the quality of rushed work may not be the best the practice can produce.

You will rarely have complete information. Situations will change. Decide what you can, when you can; then share those decisions with the project team.

And if you need to make course corrections down the road, don't fear them. Such changes usually reflect changing circumstances more than they do poor planning.

Finding the Balance

You reach a point of diminishing returns in Planning when the value you add to the project with each additional Planning hour is less than the cost of your work over that hour. The difference between the value you add with additional Planning work and its cost is called the **marginal value**. It's hard to measure Planning numerically, so the diagram at left is symbolic rather than numerical; still, keep in mind that at some point you'll need to accept that Planning, like a project, can reach the "Done" point.

Note that costs in the graph refer to the combined cost of your time plus the cost of delays on the team and on overall project value.

A faint, cold fear thrill through my veins that almost freezes up.
William Shakespeare, *Romeo and Juliet*

Project Stage 2: Planning

Nay,
PATIENCE –
or we BREAK
the sinews of our **PLOT**.

Brief #10

Checklist for Action

Watch for the following gaps:

- *Legal, between the client's situation and the desired outcome.*
- *Project, between what you know and what you need to know.*
- *Your own learning opportunities as a legal project manager.*

✓ *Gap: Resources you haven't located or that may be unavailable.*

✓ *Gap: Lack of agreement on "Done," the two or three must-do items.*

✓ *Gap: Dependencies you can't fully trace.*

✓ *Gap: Financial and budget issues*

✓ *Gap: Open (undecided) items that need action now.*

✓ *Gap: Misaligned assumptions, both project and legal.*

✓ *Gap: Unclear work process, decision-making, and conflict resolution.*

Key Takeaways

- The iron triangle of scope, schedule, and resources governs the Planning and Execution cycle. There's no free lunch; changing one element affects at least one of the others.

- Resource allocation is assigning the right people to the project's tasks, either by name or by level (e.g., "senior tax attorney").

- Create a budget to keep the costs of the work within client guidelines. Budgets guide the team as well as the project manager.

- A work breakdown structure separates the project into manageable tasks. Tasks should be no longer than ~40 hours on most projects, with a normal minimum of ~8 hours.

- Gap analysis helps you learn what you don't know, legal unknowns as well as project unknowns.

- Schedule the tasks according to resource availability, dependencies, and deadlines. (Detailed information on scheduling starts on p. 250.)

- What you don't know hurts you. Create and maintain (keep current) a risk worksheet, listing not just risks but your exposure and what you can do to mitigate or counter them.

- Watch out for analysis paralysis. Too little time in Planning leads to inefficient, costly projects. Too much leads to the same result.

Brief #11

Project Stage 3: Execution

Mountainous
ERROR
be too highly HEAPED
for truth to **OVER-PEER**.

Planning begets Execution. Execution begets surprises.

Actors in the theater rehearse long hours – their version of Planning – before they execute night after night in front of different audiences. They'll tell you that no two performances are alike. Some audiences bring energy; others enter tired and drain energy *from* the actors. One night a line that never gets a laugh will cause the audience to guffaw. Sometimes the reverse happens; a foolproof laugh line brings only silence, piercing the heart of the exposed actors.

The late Raul Julia was playing Petruchio in a New York Shakespeare Festival outdoor performance of *The Taming of the Shrew*. (It was a masterful performance, too, alongside Meryl Streep as Kate.) In a critical scene, he browbeats all about him to prove to his bride that he is master of the household. He ushers her offstage, and then returns triumphantly to share with the audience why he's acting so churlishly. It was a scene that Raul Julia pulled off wonderfully.

One evening, though, he returned, strode to the foot of the stage, but then stopped with the oddest expression. For a moment I wondered if he'd forgotten his lines. But no, it had just started to drizzle at the outdoor theater, and he knew what was about to happen to his next line:

Thus have I politicly begun my reign.

Reign. Rain. The turning point of the play, his character's key moment, was about to be mangled by an unintended laugh.

After a moment, Julia stuck out his hand to feel the raindrops and smiled. Then he delivered the line with a shrug, letting us know it was okay to giggle. Only then could he and the audience could get on with it.

In Execution, good project managers expect the unexpected; great project managers cope with it in stride.

Last night she slept not, nor tonight she shall not.
William Shakespeare, *The Taming of the Shrew*

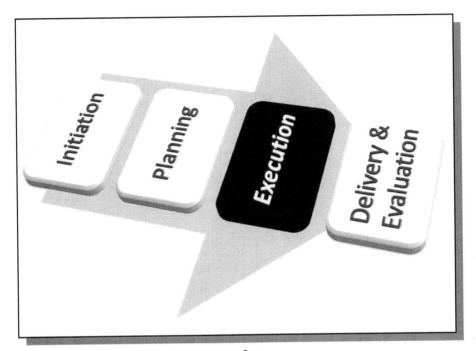

Overview: Execution

Execution is the time when mistakes large and small become apparent.

Sometimes the plan was wrong; you can't get to the North Pole by going east. Sometimes execution doesn't go according to plan; the best football game plans fail if the team keeps fumbling. Sometimes the team is asked to execute on more than is possible; one person can't do 30 hours of work in a 24-hour day. Sometimes events intervene; fog closes airports, hurricanes disrupt ports, people get sick.

No matter how much faith you put in your plans, the map is not the terrain. Execution reveals the truth.

This brief does not cover executing on the legal matter itself; the project attorneys are the experts, not I. Instead, it offers help on how to track the project during Execution; ways to spot issues and address them; and suggestions on how to handle common types of project difficulties that crop up during this stage:

- Execution overlaps Planning, minimizing your ability to stay in front of the project.

- Your client(s) are difficult to manage.

- Circumstances change.

- Circumstances differ from what you originally believed.

- You need to condense the schedule – more work than imagined, fewer or less productive resources than planned, or the client (or court, etc.) imposes new deadlines.

- The project team – or worse, the client – doesn't feel informed.

- You're having trouble ascertaining objective truth about the project.

- There's finger-pointing about failures.

All of these difficulties are common during Execution on any project, legal or otherwise. Most of them can be mitigated in advance by a project manager who understands that they can happen and who thus takes steps to prevent them. If they pop up unexpectedly, most can be handled by a project manager who stays cool under fire.

They are all foreseeable risks. You may not be able to foresee the details or exact circumstances, but the general situations recur on project after project. Some of them belong on your risk worksheet because they have specific mitigations or contingencies – e.g., schedule risks. Others such as finger-pointing are more general risks that project managers simply need to be prepared to handle.

Execution is always a team activity, even if the team is you plus the client.

A "team player" is one who makes others better.

> *To execute: that, I cannot manage alone.*
> William Shakespeare, *Henry IV pt 1*

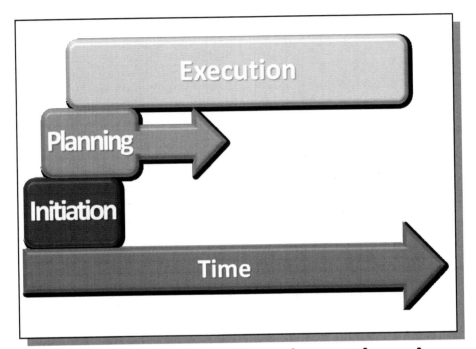

When Execution Overlaps Planning

A reality of legal projects is that Execution often begins before Planning is complete. A good project manager accepts that reality – Execution is all about accepting reality, after all – and works to minimize any ill effects.

Plan and Execute "Simpler" Tasks First

Most projects will have tasks that either require little planning or are routine. When attorneys and others on the team hunger to get started, these are great tasks to have in hand.

For example, when research is needed, the case itself may suggest the outlines of that research, even if you hold off on digging for the fine points for a time. Likewise, if a lawsuit is in the offing, there are various discovery steps that are standardized and can begin immediately; indeed, some of them, such as issuing legal holds, *must* begin immediately.

Continue Planning During Early Execution

The stages don't have hard boundaries; just because you're in Execution doesn't mean you're out of Planning. For example, you can and usually should continue to refine the work breakdown structure (p. 192) for future tasks even as the team works on current tasks. Likewise, continue scheduling future tasks (p. 190); while it's nice to have a complete schedule from the getgo, it's not essential, or necessarily congruent with reality. Risk analysis and assessment (p. 184) also continues throughout Execution.

Break Projects Into Mini-Planning/Execution Cycles

Projects can contain sub-projects. Subprojects are standard in, say, lengthy litigation: assessment, discovery, pre-trial, trial, and so on can and likely should each be their own project. You can take the same approach to shorter projects, divided roughly according to where in the timeline the pieces fall. That way, you can be planning for phase 2 while you're executing on phase 1.

Communicate Broadly and Often

There are two reasons for trying to keep Planning ahead of Execution. Of course you don't want to execute work off-target, but you also want to make sure that the team isn't duplicating work or tripping over each other.

You attack the latter problem by communicating broadly among the team, ideally using information radiators (p. 214). Ensuring that the entire team is aware of and focused on the vision and "Done" for the project also helps minimize issues of off-target work.

That is a step on which I must fall down, or else overleap.
William Shakespeare, *Macbeth*

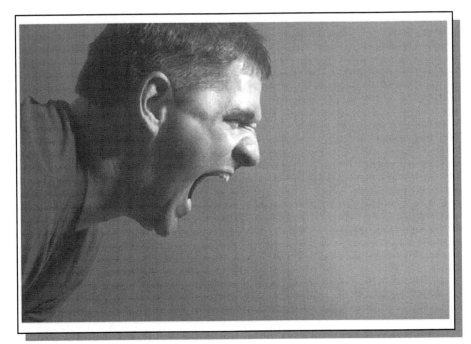

Managing Difficult Clients

For many, the least-fun project management task is dealing with a difficult client.

Clients can be needy, difficult, abusive, never satisfied.

They are also the reason for your project, and the source of the team's paycheck.

Interests and Positions

Clients have interests that are often stated as positions (p. 152). It's up to you as project manager to dig behind those positions to understand their interests. Once you understand their interests, it's a lot easier to negotiate your way to common ground, to help them see how your interests – you, your team, the practice – align with theirs – or to modify your interests to attain better alignment.

You need to understand client interests to arrive at a "Done" statement (p. 154) and develop clear conditions of satisfaction (p. 157).

Clients Aren't Mushrooms

You sometimes need to remind clients of what "Done" and success look like – not necessarily in an overt manner, but rather, "Here's the progress we're making toward what we (both) agreed our practice could do for you." The client who doesn't see the progress you're making (p. 216) is far more likely to feel abandoned and start worrying.

While there are occasional clients who enjoy tormenting their suppliers, most do so accidentally, as a byproduct of their worry or fear. After all, they're normally the expert, and now they're putting their future in your hands, in a world filled with language and rules that they don't understand.

Clients aren't mushrooms. You can't expect a good outcome keeping them in the dark and occasionally shoveling some you-know-what over them.

Hidden Stakeholders

Client organizations often have hidden stakeholders, people you don't see who have significant sway over the matter, the client lead, or both. Some client leads work for micromanagers, or worse, seagull managers (who fly in from time to time to dump on projects). Others have subordinates or peers playing office politics, trying to advance by subtly undermining the client lead. Maybe these other players honestly believe the client isn't doing the right thing and they're trying to help rather than harm. Whatever the case, you must identify these crypto-players, ferret out their interests, and seek ways to support those interests.

Why may not that be the skull of a lawyer?
William Shakespeare, *Hamlet*

Adapting to Changed Circumstances

In the O.J. Simpson murder trial, Simpson famously tried on the glove said to be found at the scene; for whatever reason, it appeared not to fit, which Simpson and his attorneys played up. It was an unpleasant surprise for the prosecution.

Apollo 13 was on its way to the moon; an explosion caused a potentially fatal loss of oxygen. It was an unpleasant surprise, to say the least.

When circumstances change, a project manager must react – calmly. The first step is to assess the new reality, because you must deal with what is rather than what you expected. In the Simpson trial, the prosecution never erased the indelible image of Simpson holding up those gloves that looked so short and tight. Apollo 13's Houston project managers and ground controllers jury-rigged a solution to save the astronauts' lives.

It doesn't matter whether the world has changed since you made project plans, or whether the world simply doesn't look the way you anticipated. Either way, no battle plan survives contact with the enemy.

"It Is What It Is"

Waste no time bemoaning the change in circumstances; such surprises are part of project management life. Instead:

---

1. Get confirmation from others that the circumstances have changed as you think they have, or as reported to you.

2. Check your risk worksheet to see if you already have a contingency plan in place.

3. Let the project team know about the new circumstances – and that you're working on adapting the project to them.

4. Deal with reality, not with what you envisioned.

If the change is significant, inform the stakeholders. If there's a significant change in plans, change management (below) offers a plan to keep stakeholders in the loop. However, even if there is little effect on the project plan, stakeholders aware of the new circumstances need to know that you're on the job, that you've got it handled.

Above all, tell the truth. Unlike wine, bad news does not get better with age.

Invoking Change Management

Most of the time when you encounter altered circumstances, you'll need to alter your project execution plans to fit them. Call on the project's change management system (p. 210) to help you work through the changes in a manner that builds confidence rather than unnecessary disruption.

The story shall be changed; Apollo flies.
William Shakespeare, *A Midsummer Night's Dream*

Change Management

Change control is often misunderstood in project management, used as a weapon by project managers who confuse delivering a project according to plan with maximizing client value. Beating back ideas with "go file a change request" protects schedules, not client value.

Still, an overly difficult process is usually better than a willy-nilly acceptance of any proposed change that sounds like a good idea. In hourly billing arrangements, additions to scope are often subtly encouraged, since added scope equals added fees. However, scope changes may not be in the client's best interest, or the team's – they are defocusing – or the practice's.

Early on, determine your project's method of handling proposed changes. Who decides to accept a change? Who participates in that decision?

Handling Proposed Changes

The project manager should set up a clear – and easy – procedure for dealing with proposed changes, called "change requests." A procedure doesn't mean a form, or hoops to jump through; rather, it's a series of steps:

1. Track the proposed change – in a spreadsheet, a project management system, even on index cards if you prefer. The project manager, not the requestor, should handle this step.

2. Investigate the ramifications of the change – cost, schedule, other disruptions v. client value, practice fiscal health.

3. Explore variants of high-value changes that might deliver most of the value with much less effort.

4. Invoke the change-decision process.

5. Inform involved parties, including the requestor.

Making Decisions

The overall project requires a clear method for making decisions (p. 244); the change process needs similar clarity. Changes are often contentious, they affect project value, costs, and schedules, and they disrupt the team. Employ a RACI or equivalent model (p. 245) for change decisions – Responsible, Approver, Consulted, Informed.

Most of all, don't forget the "informed" part. People who hear of changes through the grapevine become disenchanted and even obstructionist; it's human nature.

Changes of different magnitude may have different thresholds. Some changes require full stakeholder signoff; others can be handled at lower levels. Consider the fiscal, schedule, and disruption implications.

What means his grace, that he hath changed?
William Shakespeare, *Henry VI pt 1*

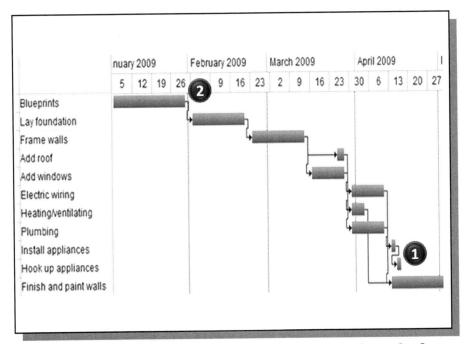

Condensing (Crashing) the Schedule

Trying to shorten the remainder of a schedule when tasks run late –
called crashing the schedule – is a thorny but necessary task for project
managers during Execution. You have a number of difficult choices:

Rearranging tasks: The easiest solution is to rearrange tasks. Note the
two appliance tasks in the slide (dot #1). Hooking up the appliances
requires both the plumber (for the dishwasher) and electrician to have
finished their other work, but they could be *installed* earlier. If the
electrician is running late, you could move the install task with minimal
impact. This solution isn't always available, however.

Splitting tasks: Sometimes you can split a task between resources. If one
associate is doing research for four days and the task's on the critical
path, could two associates each do two days of research simultaneously?

Eliminating slack time: Occasionally there's slack (unused) time in a schedule. Eliminate it when you have to, but remember that other projects may have scheduled your resources during those times.

Working extra hours: Sometimes you can ask attorneys to work additional hours during the week or on a weekend. Often, however, they're already maxed out. This is the traditional legal answer – work more hours! – but it isn't a cure-all. Also, studies show productivity goes down as hours go up. Depending on how your practice is set up, there may or may not be a cost impact to the project.

Adding resources to tasks: Some tasks can be sped up by adding resources. This differs from splitting a task in that you're adding additional hours rather than dividing a constant number of hours. You might also be able to utilize faster but more expensive (e.g., more senior) resources. These approaches can have a cost impact.

If you add resources or bill/charge back additional hours, consider the marginal costs when determining which tasks to compress. In the slide, assume the blueprints (dot #2) are late. You want to speed up either the foundation or the framing. If cement workers cost $200/day and carpenters $300/day, the marginal cost of the former is more favorable – assuming they're both equally available, rarely true in the real world.

Cutting scope: You generally can't crash the schedule without either adding resources (or working longer hours) or adjusting scope, as per the rule of the iron triangle (p. 172). Cutting scope is the least desired fix... and all too often the only realistic fix available to the project manager. Use your change management process – and involve all stakeholders – if cutting scope seems the only alternative. Give them options if you can of *where* to cut scope – and of whether they'd rather run late instead.

Communicate progress and status regularly! Make sure you establish credibility – and convey the fact that you are making real progress – *before* you run late.

The griefs are ended by seeing the worst, which late on hopes depended.
William Shakespeare, *Othello*

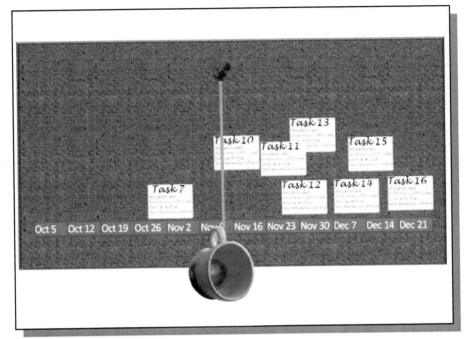

Information Radiators

An information radiator is a place where team members can view the current state of the project: schedules, tasks, progress, issues, etc. Team members can see what they need when they need it, rather than waiting for status reports or having to dig through multiple sources.

It requires neither effort nor forethought to see how things are going when the team has access to an information radiator. It's large and can be understood at a glance. And because the information changes over time, the radiator offers incentive for repeat viewing.

The original information radiators were hallway displays. Team members get an all-up view of progress – and a reminder – every time they walk by. As powerful and information-rich as such displays are, client confidentiality concerns may limit their use in the legal environment. Still, if you can dedicate a "war room" on large projects, information radiators are the way to go.

"Information radiator" is a fancy name for simple shared data, in effect the basis of knowledge management systems. Microsoft SharePoint, for example, is commonly used as a type of electronic information radiator, providing a central place where those working on or supervising a case can find the various documents associated with it. Most existing legal knowledge management systems can also fill this role quite well. With electronic (software) information radiators, consider different levels of visibility and access – team, practice, client – for different facets of project data on extended projects.

Email, of course, is another common way of sharing information. It provides a history – albeit not an organized or ordered one – of who has committed to what, by when, along with statements of what they've delivered. Email, however, is better as a retrospective information source than as a proactive information tool.

One famous software project tracked progress not on a computer but on a corkboard. The project manager put up a timeline and wrote each of the tasks and its assigned resource on an index card. Then the team hung a dirty coffee cup on a string, and moved it each day as a "You Are Here" indicator. They pulled completed tasks off the board, and so any task left hanging to the left of the coffee cup was clearly behind schedule. Everyone saw the same data, and they worked as a team to address whatever the issue was.

The slide at left shows a mock-up of the coffee-cup system (I've never been able to find an actual picture). It provides a very-easy-to-grasp snapshot of progress, making obvious any undone tasks in danger of falling behind. It's still surprising how hard it is to reproduce something that simple in software.

I can't say enough for these types of information radiators. Everyone on the team sees the same thing... including the manager.

Most radiant, exquisite, and unmatchable.
William Shakespeare, *Twelfth Night*

Proactive Progress Reporting

Unlike wine, bad news does not get better with age.

If you're building a house, you can stop by every week or two to check on progress, to see what's new since your last visit. Business leaders see regular sales reports, and they know how to view sales numbers against predictions. What do legal clients see? Of that, what do they understand?

Sometimes, the client manager will send a progress report with a monthly bill, though too often the bill is sent with tenths-of-an-hour detail but without big-picture context.

It's your job to keep stakeholders up to date on progress – weekly or biweekly, not monthly – in a way they can understand. In the absence of a story, people will make up their own – inaccurately and unfavorably.

Good progress reports are short and focused; are similar in format week after week (or fortnight after fortnight); are positive but not unduly optimistic in tone; direct support someone whose work during the reporting period has added more value than expected; and cover schedule and budget progress, any deliverables during the period, and significant issues or risks.

Progress reports are not simply listings of tasks and progress; they're your chance to convey truth about the project. They also remind stakeholders of the project vision and "Done" statement – not only keeping the focus on the long-term or strategic goal but also reminding clients with multiple projects which project is which.

Models for Progress Reporting

3 x 3 x 3 is the simplest model, listing three accomplishments (or progress items) since the last report, three items you expect to accomplish by the next report, and up to three issues that the case or project is wrestling with. *Benefits:* succinct, simple to produce, easy comparison with previous report. *Downside:* can be hard to frame items and issues in a way that makes sense to lay clients.

Tabular reports have a series of regular items (left column) for which you'll report progress. The next column lists the progress for each item. (A variant keeps the previous columnar reports to the right and inserts a new "column B" for each periodic update.) *Benefits:* Easy to maintain and fill in once the left column is set up, can map to high-level work breakdown structure (p. 192). *Downside:* Gives undue visual weight to items on which no progress was made – even when there was no work scheduled against that item during the reporting period.

Narrative reports are the hardest to write because each essentially starts from scratch. Narratives are effective on short-duration projects. Keep them short, a few paragraphs. Use separate communications to expound on any particular problems or legal issues you might be encountering.

In all the progress, both of my life and office, I have labored.
William Shakespeare, *Measure for Measure*

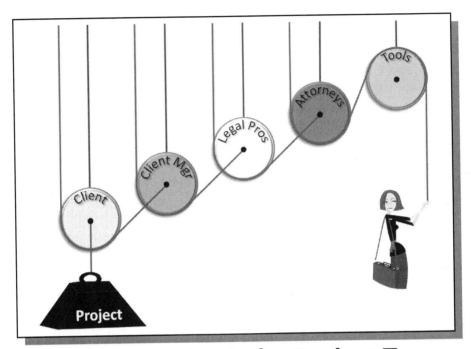

Get the Most From the Project Team

Any project is only as solid as the team executing on it.

You're the project manager; it's your (virtual) team. Whether you realize it or not, the team is looking to you for guidance. They need your assurance that the project is manageable, and that there is a clear and achievable path to success.

Keep in mind that a project team has many "moving parts" beyond the attorneys working directly on the case. There's the client manager, client lead, and other stakeholders. There may be paralegals and secretaries supporting the attorneys. There is also the intellectual challenge of the case itself, bolstered by the tools – software and otherwise – that you're using to effect and organize the project. These are all levers the project manager can use to deliver better results for both client and practice.

Project Manager or Project Leader?

In business, a manager manages tasks; a leader leads people.

It's easy for a project manager to take up the former role – there's no shortage of tasks to manage, schedules to plan, and risks to manage, while at the same time handling your individual legal responsibilities on the case. However, a project manager in the Legal Project Management world must also be a leader – communicating effectively, negotiating the best route through conflicts or unrealistic expectations, keeping the team focused on "Done" and on the right level of detail (depth v. breadth, p. 173). If an attorney is "stuck" on a problem, be a sounding board if you're a peer or even a bit junior, or be a coach if you're more knowledgeable.

Recent studies have shown that medical malpractice suits correlate strongly with poor bedside manner; given similar outcomes, the doctors who get sued the most are those who are least forthcoming with their patients. Learn from these studies: communicate directly and honestly with the project team, with the client, and with the variety of stakeholders. That, too, is project leadership.

An effective leader freely delivers praise for work well done and celebrates successes (p. 236) large and small. Positive feedback should be more plentiful than suggestions for improvements, or reminders of what remains to be done. Praise in public, but suggest or remind in private. People will work harder to live up to their praise, especially public praise; public takedowns lead to resentment, wasted energy, and locked-in thinking.

Most people do at least slightly better work when there is some pressure on them. Such pressure is best applied in the form of approaching deadlines, pride in one's work, and the need to avoid letting the team down. The last is a powerful lever indeed – but only to the extent that the worker feels an accepted, important part of a strong team.

Have you any levers to lift me up?
William Shakespeare, *Henry IV pt 1*

Outcome-Determinative Work

Related to the breadth v. depth issue (p. 173) is the notion of focusing only on outcome-determinative work.

In the model of billing by the hour, all billable work is valuable, benefiting the practice. Likewise, some in-house counsel might drive the appearance of irreplaceable value by being busy all the time, whether or not that work is adding significant value in support of client business objectives.

However, in today's model of efficient, value-based legal practice (p. 22), weigh each task against the value it delivers. Given limited time, an attorney must select the tasks that deliver the *most* value. Consider the opportunity cost (p. 134) of the tasks you *don't* take on: what else could you do with the hours/money you're thinking of devoting to a given task?

Will It Matter?

The most important tasks are those that an attorney believes will affect the outcome of a case, the outcome-determinative work. You don't always know which items will be outcome-determinative; attorneys need to enlist their professional judgment.

For example, if you were preparing your house for sale and could do only one task, would you install granite countertops in the kitchen or put most of your furniture in storage? Smart sellers seek professional (realtor) advice. Surprisingly, most realtors would say that de-cluttering the house is outcome-determinative in a way remodeling the kitchen is not. (Most buyers want rooms that feel "bigger," while many would just as soon remodel the kitchen themselves to suit their lifestyle.) There's no guarantee a particular buyer will be more excited by larger rooms than by modern countertops, but it makes sense to choose the most likely course.

Likewise, you can't guarantee that a given item will have a significant effect on the outcome. However, there are numerous mini-tasks that you could do, threads you could pursue, that you're fairly sure will *not* change the outcome. Such tasks run up bills and hours. In a firm's fixed-fee case, these tasks eat into practice profitability; in house, they curtail your ability to support more clients or more matters.

As a project manager, be on the lookout for attorneys who allow their days to be consumed with such tasks. It's difficult to make the transition from billable hours (or be-busy-all-the-time) to value-based work. The gravitational pull emanating from a comfort zone is a powerful attractant for those working in a new and challenging model.

The project manager at a firm may do well to let the client know (directly or through the client manager) about all the work you're not doing that's saving the client money, so that the client will repay with future cases.

Determine what we shall do.
William Shakespeare, *King John*

Truth, Failure, and Fault

Truth is a precious commodity on a project under pressure.

The issue is not one of attorneys or other team members lying; rather, truth gets shaded. "I'm almost done with this task," says one team member, and indeed he believes what he says, yet objectively there remains significant work on it. "This is the best compromise we'll get on these terms," says another, beaten down by a hardball negotiator.

The biggest source of untruth for a project manager, though, is... you. After a time, you start seeing what you want to see, what you expect to see; it's like proofreading your own work late at night.

The two best truth sera are a good night's sleep and the project charter. Don't evaluate or form opinions in the heat of the moment if you can help it, and refer all actions and decisions against a copy of the project charter kept in front of you. (Don't rely on your memory in this case, no matter how good it is.)

Get out of your office and talk to people in their own – face to face when possible. Celebrate the sharing of difficult truths rather than reacting in the face of them; praise the messenger. Ask open-ended questions... and listen to the answers. Use the "sniff test." And tell the truth yourself, as you know it, when you know it.

Failure happens – on tasks, on entire projects sometimes. Never take failure as a personal attack on your credibility or skills; doing so causes you to react to the person rather than the event. While no one likes or welcomes failure, remember that you learn far more from examined failures than from successes.

Fault or blame are not high-value aspects of failures. Nothing destroys a team faster than finger-pointing. If something goes wrong, you as project manager need to acknowledge the failure on behalf of the team and sometimes the practice.

Note too that often cases fall short of goals because there are multiple parties to every matter, not all of them part of the project team. You can influence a jury during a trial, but you cannot control what happens in the jury room. A patent examiner may reject even the best-written application. The other party may never have really wanted the deal to go through, or they've been playing you against someone else. In all these examples, note that the *project* may be successful even though the *case* outcome wasn't the one hoped for. You can't guarantee success; you can only work to enable it.

Risk management (p. 184) and truth are your buffers against project failure. Never be surprised by unforeseen events. Seeing and preparing for them is no guarantee of avoiding them, but it's your best chance.

Mountainous error be too highly heaped for truth to over-peer.
William Shakespeare, *Coriolanus*

Project Stage 3: Execution

Mountainous
ERROR
be too highly **HEAPED**
for truth to **OVER-PEER**.

Brief #11

Checklist for Action

If you need to condense (crash) the schedule, consider these options:

✓ *Rearrange tasks to get some off the critical path.*

✓ *Split tasks among two or more people – same total hours, but now work can happen in parallel.*

✓ *Eliminate slack time... if you have any.*

✓ *Work extra hours, but within reason; it's a legal-world tradition and often expected, but it's not a cure-all.*

✓ *Add resources to critical-path tasks – either more resources, or more expensive but faster ones.*

✓ *When none of the above will work, discuss cuts in scope with the client.*

Key Takeaways

- When Execution overlaps Planning, as it often will, execute simpler tasks first, continue Planning during early Execution, break projects into mini-Planning/Execution cycles, and communicate broadly.

- It's up to the project manager to deal with difficult clients, directly or through a client manager. Focus on their interests and how "Done" will further those interests; don't get stuck on their positions.

- Watch for hidden stakeholders, in particular in business-client organizations.

- When circumstances change or differ from what you originally believed, deal with reality. Now.

- Use change management to control the possibility of runaway projects. Make sure you have a decision structure for dealing with changes before you're confronted by them.

- You sometimes need to condense the schedule – there's more work than imagined, fewer or less productive resources than planned, or the client (or court, etc.) imposes new deadlines.

- Keep the project team and the client informed. Use information radiators to share project-team information. Provide regular progress updates, not just bills or chargeback statements, to the client.

- Seek objective truth about the project, always. Tell the truth yourself, as you know it, when you know it.

- Don't point fingers on failures. As the project manager, don't let others point fingers, either; interpose yourself if necessary.

Brief #12

Project Stage 4: Delivery and Evaluation

Note
what **TIME** we shall
our CELEBRATION
KEEP.

Most team sports often end with the winning team holding onto the ball, waiting for time to expire. In soccer, the defense tries to play "keep-away" for the final few minutes. In basketball, a guard may dribble aimlessly, watching the clock. In football, the quarterback kneels down to run time off the clock.

Baseball, however, always has a final play. There is an affirmative catch or strikeout, or else a runner crossing the plate with the winning run. There's no clock, but a final play. Only about baseball could Yogi Berra utter the immortal words, "It ain't over till it's over."

Yogi could have been a project manager.

Well-run projects don't trail off; the project manager doesn't kneel down or dribble out the clock. Rather, there should be an act of completion, a "Done" moment at which the practice and the client agree affirmatively that the project is complete. It could be a phone call, a handshake, even an email, but there should be some clear dividing line between "in the project" and "done with the project."

It's more than a formality. It is an agreement with the client that "Done" has been achieved, that the conditions of satisfaction have been met. It is also an acknowledgement to the project team of their hard work and a reminder that they are now formally released from case-related responsibilities on this project.

There's still a bit of work after that final moment. There may be a bill to be sent or a chargeback to be posted. More importantly, there should be a post-project evaluation – what went well, what could have gone better, what we individually and collectively might learn that we can apply to future projects.

Until then, it ain't over.

This have I thought good to deliver.
William Shakespeare, *Macbeth*

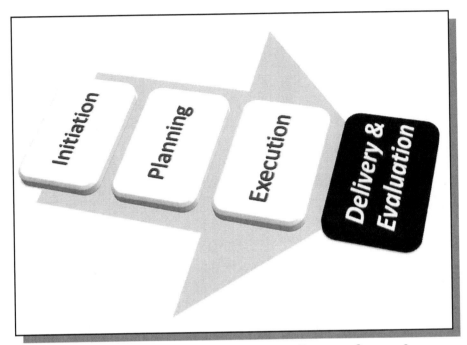

Overview: Delivery and Evaluation

In traditional project management, Delivery and Evaluation may be separate stages, especially when Delivery is an extended process – say, a rollout of a project to multiple users. However, in the provision of services – and thus Legal Project Management – the Execution stage really represents the continuous delivery of work. A last step of Delivery tends more toward a snapshot – a completed contract, say – than an extended stage. As with building a house, there is a moment when the client receives the keys, at least symbolically.

Delivery

Delivery marks the last chance for the project manager to ensure that the client is happy – not just satisfied, but delighted – with the work the practice has done on her behalf. Any client grumbling should be addressed before it has the chance to blossom into dissatisfaction with the practice and the work you've done.

Just as you obtained signoff from the stakeholders on the project charter (p. 158), you should obtain signoff that the project is complete. Sometimes, "complete" may have to be "substantially complete," potentially subject to a "punch list" of minor items (p. 231). In either case, you're marking a substantive end to both the project and the matter (or to the phase in a lengthy matter divided into multiple projects).

Evaluation

Just as projects begin with at least a minimal Evaluation, so should they end with Evaluation. The initial Evaluation, rolled into Initiation in Legal Project Management, asks, "Should we do this project?" The closing Evaluation asks, "How well did we do on this project – and what did we learn?"

In many systems this stage has acquired the unfortunate name "post mortem." That name embeds the idea of failure – "after death" – into the very structure of the project; projects can be tough enough without a subliminal suggestions that the final stage will discuss its failure.

Rather, Evaluation should be a time for celebration (p. 236): celebrate the likely success, celebrate the work itself, celebrate what you and the project team have learned during the course of the project.

Loose Ends

In addition to a possible punch list, there may be other items that the project manager must look to on concluding the project. For example, make sure that documents and knowledge have been captured in whatever solution you may use for these purposes (p. 232). Highly successful projects may also have completion bonuses to be worked out.

I have already delivered.
William Shakespeare, *Much Ado About Nothing*

Embrace a Conclusion

One of the project manager's last jobs on a project is to lead the transition from active to completed project. Omitting this transition results in lost opportunities.

Signoff

Signoff is more than client acknowledgment that the project is complete, or substantially complete (see below). It is a chance to confirm with the client that you have met the conditions of satisfaction (p. 157) and the client is pleased with the practice's work.

First, obtaining the client's assent that the work is complete will prevent the growth of last-minute "one more thing" items that can snatch fixed-fee defeat from the jaws of victory. Second, it's a chance to gauge "repurchase intent." For firms, you want to increase the likelihood that the client will use your services on future projects; in-house performance evaluations often depend on feedback from those you work with. In either case, signoff is your chance to assuage any nagging doubts that might grow untended into future reluctance. "I can't put my finger on it, but I just didn't have a good experience with them" is the way businesses lose customers even when things seem to be going well.

Survey

Nowadays, it's hard to escape the follow-up survey when you buy something on line. Surveys offer three things: the chance to make things right; feedback that will improve future offerings; and a small additional bond between buyer and seller/client.

Practices can send a formal, standardized feedback survey to client stakeholders on project delivery; while such surveys aren't common, they do send the message that you take feedback seriously. With or without a survey, the client manager or project manager should have telephone or face-to-face conversations with client stakeholders for the three reasons noted above.

The Punch List

With a new house, there is usually a short period after completion – formally called "substantially complete" – where buyer and builder maintain a "punch list." A punch list is a tally of minor items that the builder must still attend to – nicks in the molding, say, or a lighting fixture that remains backordered.

Likewise, there may be a punch list for a legal project if there are minor items still outstanding. It is up to the project manager to maintain that punch list and ensure that each of those items is completed in a way that maintains client satisfaction.

From east, west, north, and south be it concluded.
William Shakespeare, *The Winter's Tale*

Save It! DM and KM Systems

Attorneys are knowledge workers. They trade on what they know rather than, say, the labor of their hands.

All practices have some form of document management (DM) and knowledge management (KM) systems, whether they recognize it or not. The old-style filing cabinet is very much a DM system. So is the hard drive on a desktop computer, no matter how organized or disorganized the documents may be. Increasingly sophisticated and powerful software solutions are becoming more common, providing additional levels of organization and categorization and search and retrieval capabilities.

Practices have stated or tacit norms on DM systems. Project managers can urge the project team toward computer-based solutions, but unless they're supported by practice norms, compliance will be low.

The project completion period marks one last opportunity to capture project documents in the practice's formal system. As project manager you probably have access to all or most of the documents generated during the project; it may be up to you (or a person supporting you, such as a legal secretary) to make up for others on the team who aren't regular users of such solutions. While it would be better if all of the attorneys made use of these solutions, this may not be the most important battle you have to fight – so for the good of the practice, pick up the slack yourself.

There's a crossover between KM and DM. Documents such as buyer and seller first drafts, due diligence checklists, and so on fit both categories.

Fear of Sharing

Knowledge management is harder than document management. The latter deals with tangible items, or at least with the electrons that represent these tangible items today. The former is an attempt to capture what's in the attorney's head.

KM at a practice may consist of knocking on a senior attorney's door, or asking a colleague, "Who's our expert on X?" However, an increasing number of practices are installing KM solutions, and some even have senior leaders applying pressure to encourage use of such solutions.

Unfortunately, many attorneys still hoard their knowledge, believing it gives them an edge in retaining future billings. Knowledge hoarding is common in the business world as well as the legal sphere; it's a play for power in the office, often without the hoarder's conscious recognition.

As project manager, you have two duties with respect to KM:

1. Encourage the team to share what they've learned to a level at least consistent with practice standards.

2. Share your own knowledge and learnings from the project.

How prove you that, in the great heap of your knowledge?
William Shakespeare, *As You Like It*

Learn From Experience: Debriefing

At the end of every space mission, every military mission, and most projects, the leaders debrief the participants. Leaders know that the way to avoid duplicating previous mistakes, the way to get smarter as an organization, is to learn what went wrong, and right, on each mission.

Do the same on legal projects. Build a debriefing session into the project schedule and task list/work breakdown structure, and get it on team member calendars. While it may not do much for the project just completed, such debriefing sessions will help the *practice* considerably.

Structure of the Debriefing Session

Debriefing sessions ideally assemble the team one last time to discuss:

- What went right, and what team members learned from it.

- What didn't go as well. Speakers should note their understanding of the reasons, along with steps they'll take to keep similar problems from recurring on future projects.

- What they learned from the project.

In strongly functioning teams, these sessions work well with the team gathered in a room, face to face. However, significant power disparities (e.g., senior attorney and legal secretary) or ill will among team members will stifle the open exchange of ideas – or turn it into a gripe session with team members attacking each other. (You know which end of the arrow the project manager will usually face.)

Thus it's often a good idea to request responses in advance of the meeting to the three items above. Summarize the responses, remove the author's name and specific references to others on the team, and circulate the report ahead of the meeting. Note who isn't speaking up at the meeting; consider talking briefly with them later in private to see if they're willing to offer feedback in a less exposed setting.

If you suspect that team members would prefer to be anonymous even with regard to sharing their thoughts with you, use one of the many free online survey tools to collect responses.

Debrief meetings work best in person (or with large-format telepresence). However, it's not always possible to gather the team in person, whether because they work in multiple locations or because it's impossible to schedule a time where they're all free. Meet with whomever you can, and seek additional feedback from everyone via survey or email.

Report out to the team on your findings – including your own learnings.

Strongly consider inviting the client to attend debriefing sessions.

Yes, I have gained my experience.
William Shakespeare, *As You Like It*

Celebrate Success

Celebrating success involves more than taking the project team to Morton's Steakhouse after Delivery.

That's a good start – or rather, a good finish. Human transitions are marked by passage ceremonies: graduation, bar mitzvah, first communion, wedding, and so on. The team will welcome a tangible celebration to conclude a project, whether dinner at a nice restaurant or a cake shared at the Evaluation debriefing session. It is a reminder that the practice values the work just concluded and that the work *is* concluded, the client's business bettered thanks to the team's efforts.

Small Victories = Important Victories

It's not the reward at the end that truly drives progress, however.

Maslow's hierarchy of needs posits esteem as a major factor in human behavior; we need both the respect of others and the self-esteem earned by mastery and competence. Succeeding on tasks within a project supports both of these esteem-related needs.

Blanchard and Johnson, in *The One-Minute Manager*, popularized the phrase, "Catch them doing something right." It's a simple concept too often ignored by managers, but easily available to a project manager willing to leave his office. Find someone on the project team making progress on an item, offer thanks and praise, and spend 30 seconds sharing with her the specific value her work is adding and/or what in particular she's doing so well. Sometimes you can do this spontaneously; other times, you can act in response to some work that the team member has just submitted, or even a particular insight she just offered.

Can you do it by email? Email lacks the immediacy and personal touch, but with a distributed team it may be the tool best suited to the job. However, email does offer an easy way to offer public praise and support; send a note expressing your thanks or appreciation when the team member supplies something needed for the project or completes a task. Copy the rest of the team on the note, along with the person's manager. There's no easier way to build support.

When someone comes through with an extra special result or extraordinary effort, you can also thank him by sending a brief note to his manager – or even his manager's manager if that's what it takes to reach a partner or AGC. There is some danger of overdoing the praise and rendering it meaningless; however, it's more common that people forget to do this at all.

Be specific: "Thanks for getting the redlining done and collating all the changes. You've helped us create a version acceptable to all parties, and gained a day on the schedule in the bargain." That's all it takes.

Never forget to celebrate success out loud, for victories both small and large.

Note what time we shall our celebration keep.
William Shakespeare, *Twelfth Night*

Project Stage 4: Delivery and Evaluation

Note

what **TIME** we shall

our **CELEBRATION**

KEEP.

Brief #12

Checklist for Action

At the debriefing session, seek the following feedback:

✓ *What went right.*

✓ *What team members learned from what went right.*

✓ *What didn't go well.*

✓ *How you can learn and improve in areas that didn't go well.*

✓ *What team members learned from the substantive work itself.*

• Face to face meetings are best. Ensure that they stay productive and that even subtle personal attacks are blocked before they begin.

• Get input from team members up front. Anonymize and distribute it before the debriefing.

• Seek out separately those unwilling to give feedback in public.

Key Takeaways

- Don't forget that Delivery and Evaluation is an important finishing stage to every project.

- People need closure. Acknowledge the need.

- Obtain signoff from stakeholders that the project has reached "Done" and that the practice has met the conditions of satisfaction.

- Some projects may wind up with a "punch list" of minor items before you can close them. "Substantially complete" is a legitimate milestone and transition marker.

- Ask the client for feedback about the project. Even the simple act of requesting feedback – and hearing the client out – improves client satisfaction. It's even better if you find value in the feedback and use it to improve future work.

- Make sure project documents make it into your document management solution, whatever that may be: filing cabinet, email folder, formal software program.

- Capture as much knowledge and learning as you can in the practice knowledge management solution, even if that amounts to an informal sharing of lessons learned.

- Hold a debriefing session as part of Evaluation. Learn what went well and how you can build on it. Learn what didn't go so well, and draw lessons on how to improve those aspects on future projects.

- Celebrate project success with some sort of passage ceremony. It needn't be an expensive team dinner; on small projects, a sincere "thank you for a job well done" can be meaningful.

- Celebrate individual successes. Provide positive, specific feedback when you catch someone doing something right. Let the team share in successes by publicly acknowledging progress.

BEYOND...

...WHY, WHAT, WHO, WHEN, WHERE, HOW

Reporters first ask the six basic questions, and consider the answers.

Then they select a few facets of the story. Into these they dig deeper.

Brief #13

Practical LPM

The path
is **SMOOTH**
that LEADETH
on to **DANGER**.

The first hole on my favorite golf course is a short par 3, 147 yards. However, between tee and green are two lovely evergreens, 70 or 80 feet tall, trunks bare but with crowns of green branches that reach toward each other to form a wall, guarding the green.

A good tee shot, hit with a lofted iron, soars over the evergreens and comes to rest easily on the green.

I hit a shot like that once. Sure enough, it stopped two feet from the hole, the only birdie I'd ever gotten on the hole. But I'm not a very good golfer. Most of my tee shots over the years hit the branches and dropped sadly to the ground under the trees. Like any bad golfer, I kept trying to hit it harder to clear the trees, now adding to my arsenal a bunch of shots that wound up in the bushes left of the fairway or out of bounds hopping down the road on the right. Frustrated by my increasing lack of success, and pressured by my sense that people in the clubhouse could witness my futility, each week I'd try harder and get worse.

One day, playing with my then eight-year-old son, I made my usual hash of it. He took out his driver, his biggest club. He could hit it 120 to 130 yards, just about the distance from the forward tees, so he had no worries about smashing it too far. He hit the ball on the nose – a line drive that landed on the edge of the green after passing low *between* the trees.

He didn't worry about what he was supposed to do, or what the course designer intended as the "right" approach to the hole. He just found a very practical solution, one he's been able to repeat almost every time we play the course together.

That's how I play it now, ending on the green more often than not. Not elegant, but practical – practical and effective.

Effective project management is practical project management.

There's something in it, more than my father's skill.
William Shakespeare, *All's Well That Ends Well*

	Responsible Accountable		Consulted Informed			
	Client Manager	Lead Attorney	Case Attorneys	Para- legals	Client Lead	Forensic Specialist
Case Strategy	A	R	C	I	C	I
Discovery Request	I	A	R	I	I	C
Production Analysis		A	R		I	C
Meet and Confer	A	R	C		C	R

Making Decisions

How will you make decisions on this project? That's a harder question than it appears. Commonly more than one person thinks he "owns" a decision. Even if such disputes don't come out into the open, they lead to backbiting, low morale, and sniping at the project, situations a project manager can't afford.

Determine at the start of a project who owns what types of decisions – and how you will determine who owns decisions in areas you hadn't considered. Deciding about decision-making itself applies both to the case as well as the project surrounding the case.

You need to decide who makes what decisions; how to make them; and when to make them. Which decisions benefit from early direction? Which are better after you've had time to let the facts settle?

Case (Legal) Decisions

Who will make significant decisions about case direction? The client lead? The lead attorney? Her manager? The GC? What if you've brought on a specialist for a particular aspect of the case? Should he make the call in his specialty, or does it need to be approved by someone with a broader view of the overall case? It's better to figure this out up front than to scramble when you need a decision.

Project Decisions

Generally, the project manager is responsible for decisions about the project itself – how it will be run, how to handle certain risks, whom to engage, and so on. However, the client manager – the attorney directly accountable to the client – may want to review major decisions.

The RACI Model: Defining Responsibility

You can use a RACI matrix to ensure clarity on responsibilities:

- **Responsible:** The people performing the core work, usually attorneys.

- **Accountable:** The person ultimately accountable to the client. There can be many workers responsible but only one person accountable.

- **Consulted:** Those whose opinions you seek, usually actively.

- **Informed:** Those you keep up to date on progress, decisions, etc.

The slide shows a fictitious RACI matrix with each major task mapped to the various roles – who's accountable, responsible, and so on. Even in that fictitious example, note the client lead – consulted or informed, but not responsible or accountable *within the boundaries of the project.*

Watch out for difference between accountability (on the hook with the client) and responsibility (perform the work). Also, be broad-minded about whom you consult; consulting people keeps them on board.

Betwixt ourselves let us decide it.
William Shakespeare, *Henry VI pt 1*

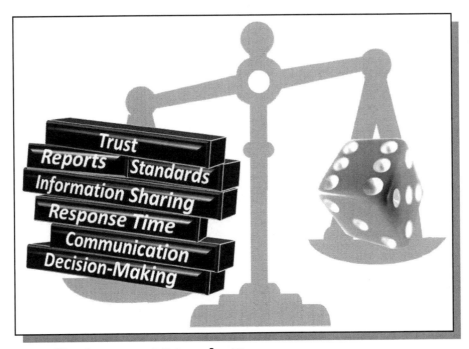

Defining a Work Process

For cases involving multiple attorneys with at least some responsibility for decisions and/or independent work, Initiation offers the opportunity to define facets of your work process.

Decision Making

The previous spread covers decision-making within the work process.

Intra-Team Communication

How will you communicate? Email? In person? Phone? Twitter? (Okay, probably not Twitter.) A common workspace, such as SharePoint or Legal OnRamp? If your practice lacks established norms, don't assume that your preferred method works for everyone.

Response Times and Availability

How quickly should the team members expect responses from each other? Keep in mind that the more interrupt-driven you are, the less total work you get done – no matter that it feels like you're busy all the time. Consider a four-hour or even one-business-day response norm for email; pick up the phone if it's both urgent and important (p. 266).

Also, are there core hours when you expect the team to be responsive? For example, I normally block out 5:30-7:30 PM for family time when I'm not traveling; my teams know they can contact me again after 7:30.

Information Sharing

Determine up front what types of information you cannot share because of confidentiality or privilege issues. How will you share the rest? A common workspace? A document management system? Email?

Reporting Up

Decide what and how often you'll report up to stakeholders (p. 216).

Standards and Tools

Are there certain technology standards you expect the team to share? Will you send documents only by PDF? Do you require a metadata scrub before sending Word files? When do you put work product into the DMS?

Trust

The sum of the facets of the work process is trust among the team members and by the stakeholders. You'll get a lot more done in an environment of trust; it's well worth the time to build that trust.

I like your work, and you shall find I like it.
William Shakespeare, *Timon of Athens*

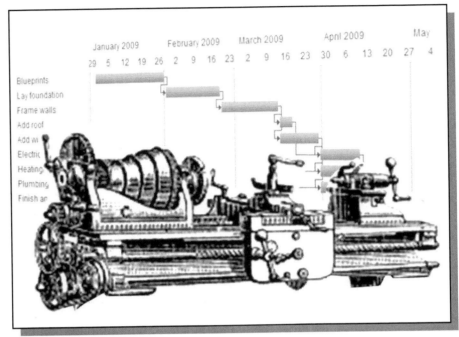

A First Look at Tools

Buying a lathe does not make you a carpenter.

It works the other way 'round, too; not all carpenters need lathes. A lathe is a highly specialized tool with limited applicability; it requires a lot of skill to run one well; and few carpentry projects actually need one. Also, you can hurt yourself with one.

I'd say the same thing about Legal Project Management. Moving prematurely to specialized, high-end project management tools can hurt your goals, doing more harm than good.

Personally, I like Microsoft Project and have used it successfully on projects large and small. However, it's a professional project manager's tool, as are its main competitors.

Type of Project Management Tools

Schedulers are what most people visualize when they think about project management. They produce a common visual schedule format (Gantt charts, p. 254 ff.), and many so-called "project management systems" open to the scheduling tool as the default. These tools allow you to easily create work breakdown structures (pp. 192, 250), assign and track dependencies (pp. 193, 252), and create schedules based on that information.

Resource managers give project scheduling solutions the added ability to track work assignments. They can track who's assigned to what tasks, adjust schedules so that team members don't have to be in two places at once, or warn you that a team member appears overloaded with work. They can also create quick project budgets if you assign costs to the resources.

Portfolio/enterprise managers can coordinate multiple projects that use the same resources. If you have Attorney A scheduled full time and another project manager also has Attorney A scheduled full time during a given period, only an analysis of the projects together will reveal the problem before Attorney A starts screaming for help... or falling behind on your project.

Related Tools and Features

Issue tracking solutions maintain flexible lists of issues across one or more project teams. While they are used mostly for software development to track bugs or contact centers and helpdesks to track user issues, some also have tools for tracking and corralling risks (p. 184).

Collaborative project management solutions allow the entire team to view, create, and alter project-related information. Both these tools and portfolio managers may require IT setup and support.

Having work more plentiful than tools.
William Shakespeare, *Cymbeline*

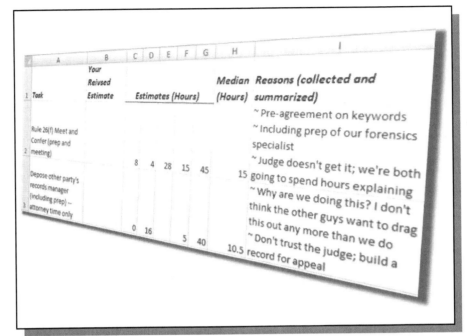

Estimating Task Length/Work

Estimating the amount of work on a task is difficult, notoriously unreliable, and surrounded by traps. Estimates are most reliable for repeatable detail-level work such as patent prosecution; they are much less so for work that is open-ended work, new, or involves other parties.

The best estimators of a task are those who will perform it. Not only do they know their own work rates, they make an implicit commitment to performing the work within their estimated time. However, you don't always know who will perform a task in advance, nor is it always possible to request their time to create an estimate.

Estimates also bring in Parkinson's Law: work expands to fill the time available for its completion. If an attorney has 30 hours allotted to a task, she is likely to dive into 30 hours of detail – even if she might have met the acceptable level of thoroughness for the task in half that time.

Thus it's important that you include depth of scope in describing or delineating tasks. Those extra hours not only represent practice profit, time saved, or both, they will likely be needed elsewhere when other tasks overrun their estimates.

Beware also the attorney seeking perfection, unwilling to let go of a task until he has explored every possible nuance. Some tasks warrant this level of depth, but many do not, especially when clients are demanding more efficacious use of their money. In addition, some people are unwilling to let go of their work; in that past, that's been a prized quality in attorneys, but it is not a strength in a cost-competitive environment.

Estimating itself is a task that consumes time; account for it in the WBS, whether you treat it as billable (chargeback-able?) or overhead.

Delphi: Estimating With Little to Go On

Sometimes no one is sure how long a task will take, or there are wildly divergent opinions. Many fields have used the Rand Corporation's Delphi technique, which builds consensus estimates from teams of experts (experienced legal professionals in our case). Each estimator examines the task information and provides an estimate along with a brief rationale. The project manager creates an anonymous summary and sends it back to the estimators, who read the comments and often revise their estimates in light of them. Over a few rounds, you build consensus. James Surowiecki has described similar approaches – and their surprising levels of accuracy – in various fields.

Include paralegals and secretaries in the estimating pools; they may have accurate observations about how long attorneys actually spend on various tasks.

It is valuable to have at least two estimates for unfamiliar tasks: expected time and pessimistic time. You can use a weighted average to create an overall estimate; some project management tools can also help.

Some oracle must rectify our knowledge.
William Shakespeare, *The Tempest*

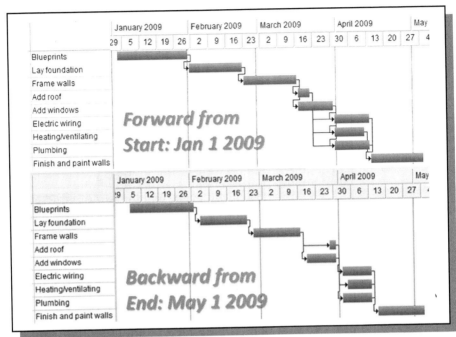

Scheduling Backward and Forward

There are basically two ways to calculate a project schedule. I'll illustrate both with a simple and superficial example, building a house.

Working From the Start: Forward Scheduling

Forward scheduling is a bit more straightforward, especially when there are complex dependencies; it's also easier if you schedule manually.

Take the start date and lay out all the tasks. If one task depends on another, don't start it until the other task finishes (subject to finish-to-start scheduling, lag or lead time, and such – see p. 252). Also beware of resource limitations/constraints; a person can't be in two places at once, or do two (full-time) tasks as the same time. In forward scheduling, tasks start as soon as possible (ASAP) unless you choose otherwise.

The top part of the slide shows the house schedule based on a start date. The scheduling program noted the dependencies – e.g., you can't do the roof until the walls are framed, although you *can* do the roof and windows at the same time.

Working Back From the Due Date: Backward Scheduling

In backward scheduling, you start with a deadline and figure out when you have to start. Tasks now start as late as possible (ALAP) unless you choose otherwise. As dependencies build up, backward scheduling can get somewhat complicated without a scheduling program.

Note the bottom schedule on the slide: we want to be in our new home by May 1. At first glance, the schedules look alike; either way, the house takes four months to build. (I warned you it wasn't realistic.) Look carefully at the roof and windows tasks. They share a dependency (framing) and now begin as late as possible; thus the roofer, who has the shorter task, doesn't have to begin until the window team is nearly done.

The roofer has slack time in either schedule; in forward scheduling, slack is placed by default after her assigned period, but in ALAP backward scheduling it occurs *in front of* that period. In truth, as long as the roofer is done by the time the window team finishes, it doesn't matter whether she starts March 16, March 25, or anytime in between.

But... what if the roofer is late? If she's scheduled to start as soon as possible, she can be a week late without affecting the schedule. However, if she starts as late as possible and misses her dates, the whole house will be late – probably months late as the plumber and electrician disappear to take other jobs.

Thus even in backward scheduling, consider starting tasks ASAP rather than ALAP. People who think they have slack tend to use it, as Ted Klastorin points out empirically and mathematically – and then delay suddenly has consequences.

Writ uncertainly by this short schedule...
William Shakespeare, *The Rape of Lucrece*

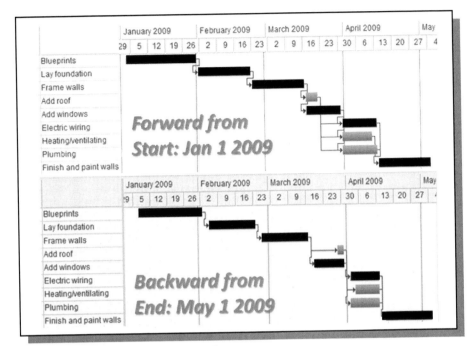

The Critical Path

In the build-a-house schedules in the slide above, the roofer has slack time; as long as she is done by the time the windows are in, she doesn't affect the move-in date. Any fenestration delays, however, ripple immediately through the rest of the project.

The windows are on the **critical path**, which is the sequence of tasks (dark bars in the slide) where any delay will hold up delivery of the entire project.

The critical path might not remain constant. If the roofer falls behind the window team, she jumps onto the critical path. Thus critical path tasks bear extra watchfulness... but don't take your eye off the others yet. Note above how small a slip would have the plumber supplant the electrician on the critical path.

Given the inaccuracy of most estimates, it's often hard to be sure which tasks truly line the critical path. Even small deviations from estimates can cause formerly "safe" tasks to pop up on the critical path.

Mitigating Critical Path Risks

The iron triangle (p.170) suggests that there are three things you can do – beyond watchfulness and encouragement – to mitigate critical path risks:

1. Cut scope. It usually takes less time to do less work.

2. Add people. (Remember the awful math problems such as "If two and a half people can paint two-thirds of a wall in four and a half hours....") However, it's a project management truism, first articulated by Frederic Brooks, that "adding people to a task that's late only makes it later." It takes time to bring new team members up to speed, there are more lines of communication that can get cross-wired, work styles on a shared task may be incompatible, and so on. Sometimes, if someone isn't working full-time on a project, you may be able to negotiate more hours each day for a time.

3. Extend the schedule. However, if you miss the train by a minute, the next may be an hour later. Be cautious extending time for critical path tasks; beware ripple effects further along in the project.

Actually, there is one more thing a project manager can do – remove roadblocks.

Fend off the distractions hammering the people on the critical path. Get them lunch or dinner, even do their shopping. If someone is on the critical path and you are not, your job is to save them time... and perhaps save your project.

The path is smooth that leadeth on to danger.
William Shakespeare, *Venus and Adonis*

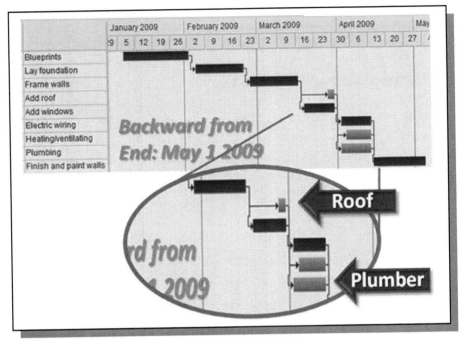

More Scheduling Angst

I include multiple spreads on scheduling because it's the default option in programs such as Microsoft Project. Project managers just starting out often fall into the trap of believing that the schedule *is* the project.

The map is not the terrain. But it's a very prominent map.

Spotting Hidden Traps

Any task on the critical path that cannot move, such as a filing date, is a high risk. Small slips can ripple down until they hit this immovable wall (cf. p. 210). Suddenly, your project is literally up against the wall. This problem can be exacerbated if your software solution for tracking, say, court dates isn't integrated with your scheduling tool.

If you create a schedule graph such as the Gantt chart at left, inspect it for tasks similar in time to critical-path tasks (e.g., plumbing is similar to electrical work) or tasks with significant slack before they start (e.g., roofing). You can also use the tool's reporting functions, but they may be complex; visual inspection is often easier. Consider what happens if the roofer is a few days late but the plumber has to be on another month-long job by April 13. Suddenly move-in is at risk because of a small slip.

The better scheduling tools allow you to create alternate schedules around different sets of estimates, often called normal, pessimistic, and optimistic times. The first is the default duration; however, tracking pessimistic times is a great way to spot problem areas in a schedule.

You can ask for pessimistic estimates as well as normal ones when you collect estimates; you can also create them yourself if you have expertise in the areas in question. While the latter method isn't exactly standard project management, attorneys aren't standard project managers.

Confirming Estimates

Once you have a work breakdown structure (p. 192), the project team should validate it. Seek each person's agreement that the estimate is reasonable for each task they'll work on. If you can sometimes bully people into committing to impossible dates, you cannot bully them into meeting those dates.

If you've created a Gantt chart such as the ones in the preceding spread (see also p. 260), it's wise to have each team member look over a list of their tasks with the scheduled dates. If you have to hear "I'll be out of town that week," you want to hear it now, not the day the task is set to start (or worse – the day it's due).

With a validated work breakdown structure (a/k/a annotated task list), you can estimate project costs (see pp. 145 and 174).

I see, as in a map, the end of all.
William Shakespeare, *Richard III*

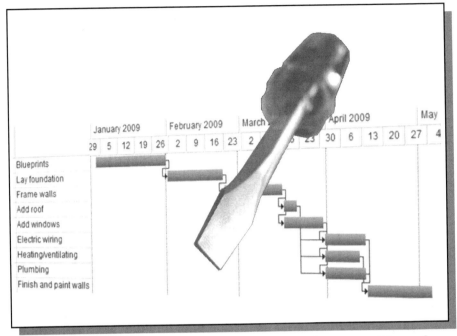

A Few More Thoughts About Tools

A carpenter sees someone using a slotted (flat-blade) screwdriver as a chisel, chipping away wood. She says, "That's the hard way, and it'll leave ugly marks; get a chisel." Or maybe she says, "Very clever, since that screwdriver is exactly the right width for what you're doing." As attorneys, say, it depends. In this case, it depends on the carpenter, the tool-wielder, and the job itself.

The Right Tool for the Right Job

Should you use a dedicated project scheduling tool such as Microsoft Project? It depends. (You knew that was coming.) A relatively novice user can probably do the following tasks easily in such a tool:

- Create a simple work breakdown structure (p. 192).

- Assign tasks to resources and track the total time and cost per team member (note: looking at resource overloading is manageable, but using the tool to guide adjustment of overloads is noticeably harder).

- Map and track dependencies (pp. 182, 252).

- Create a *simple* schedule (p. 254) to use *as a guide* (creating a full updateable schedule is harder and much more time-consuming).

There's a huge leap between basic and proficient usage of these tools. Beware of getting caught up in tool complexities; don't be afraid to fall back to spreadsheets or even whiteboards. Tools can create a schedule, but they can't make it match reality – or make the team stick to it.

Gantt Charts ("Schedules") and Tools

Task estimates are hopes, not guarantees. Just because it's on the Gantt chart doesn't mean it's accurate. The map is not the terrain. Likewise, just because sophisticated Gantt charts can show lots of detail – percent complete, task assignments, critical path, lag and slack, etc. – doesn't mean you need to enter that level of detail. The project manager should be aware of and track all of this information – but use the toolset you're most comfortable with. Don't get lost in your tools.

Pessimistic Estimates and Schedules

Schedulers allow you to enter multiple estimates for task duration, in particular most likely, optimistic, and pessimistic durations. Hitting optimistic estimates is rare; hitting or even surpassing pessimistic estimates, unfortunately, isn't at all rare.

Although it takes a bit more time, it may be worthwhile to create pessimistic estimates for tasks where either you or the assignee is unsure about the amount of work needed. Then create both most-likely and pessimistic schedules – and if the tool permits, an expected schedule that weights the two duration options in calculating a schedule.

Take you to your tools.
William Shakespeare, *Titus Andronicus*

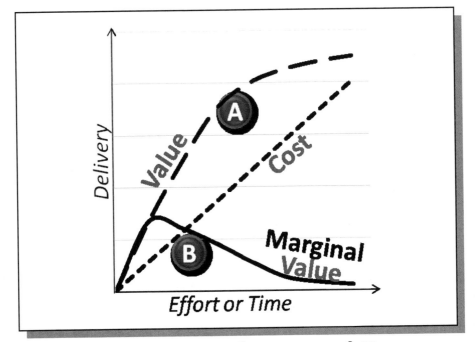

Triangulating Budgets and Fees

There are a couple of issues worth examining in developing the most effective budget using Legal Project Management.

How Much Can You Do for $X?

While a client might not ask the question this baldly – actually, some indeed might – it may be there as an undercurrent.

Consider the graph in the slide. Over time or with additional effort, the **value** you deliver to the client increases. However, at some point – say, Point A – you move from *adding* massive new value to *refining* the value you've created. You're still adding value, just not as ferociously.

Cost remains a constant; each unit of effort adds a unit of cost.

Now look at the third curve, **marginal value**: Marginal value is the value you *add* for each added unit of cost. Note that it declines after a while, as you move into *refining* the value you've previously created rather than creating significant new value. See Point B in the slide.

The marginal value curve guides your answer to the client's question of what you can do for $X. The client who wants the best work possible will move to the right end of that curve. The client who seeks a good result at a reasonable price moves to the left.

Find the balance – for the practice and the client – among total value, effort (cost), and marginal value, in effect triangulating your course. Of course, as you participate in the business of the practice, you're also considering which options make most sense for the practice's health, both short-term and long-term.

Here's a variant of this type of triangulation. You: "How important is it that we do X?" Client: "How much will it cost?" In this situation, the client is usually looking for a range: "100% coverage of legal issue X will cost $M, 40% coverage will cost $N, and so on." Again, you're working the marginal value equation with the client, balancing her benefit, the project's (case's) benefit, and the practice's benefit.

Ongoing Budget Tracking

Most law firms and some departments have a time-and-billing system. If so, you should be able to get a report at any time detailing the amount of time spent on the various project tasks, depending on how assiduous the attorneys are at entering their time.

Compare this data not only to your estimates, but also, if you're an attorney and know the subject area, to the marginal value you're delivering to the client. Be watchful for Point B (see the slide), the point of diminishing returns. In the ideal world, the attorneys on the project team would themselves be aware of the marginal value issue, recognizing the possibility of diminishing returns.

A mote will turn the balance.
William Shakespeare, *A Midsummer Night's Dream*

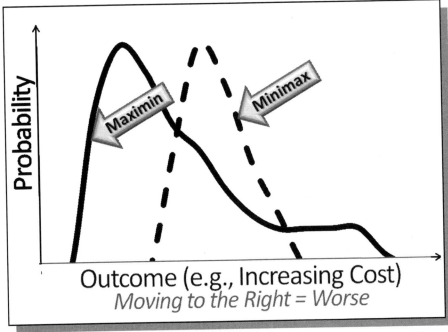

Containing Risk: Minimax, Maximin

You're heading home after a long day at work. Route 1, with traffic light after traffic light, moves at a slow, predictable pace. The trip takes an hour each time you go that way. On the other hand, Route 9 has no lights; at this hour it should take you 40 minutes. However, if it's jammed up, which happens occasionally and unpredictably, it will take you an hour and a half. Which road do you choose?

What if your daughter's school play starts in 70 minutes? Clearly, you can't afford to be late. You take Route 1, right? That's the minimax way.

What if your son's bedtime is 50 minutes away and you want the best chance to kiss him goodnight? It has to be Route 9, the maximin answer.

A minimax solution **mini**mizes the **max**imum cost, or risk. Conversely, a maximin solution **maxi**mizes the likelihood of **min**imum cost or risk.

You're might be familiar with similar decisions in legal practice. Accepting a plea bargain, for example, is a defendant's minimax solution.

The ideas behind minimax and maximin aren't themselves new to most attorneys, but these terms codify the concepts within a structure.

Applying Minimax to Project Risk

Here are some ways you can apply minimax/maximin thinking to risk.

Risk mitigation: Consider which risks you want to work hardest to mitigate. Each risk, if you create a full risk worksheet, has an expected loss, the probability of occurrence multiplied by the cost if it does occur (p. 184). The simplest approach is to focus on those with the largest expected loss. However, what if one risk has a limited – or hard to predict – likelihood but a very high cost to the case should it occur?

If you can't afford to allow this possibility or similar high-cost risks, you would take the minimax approach, minimizing the maximum loss. The downside, of course, is that you're not spending the time mitigating risks far more likely to occur, albeit with smaller consequences when they do show up.

Assigning resources: Think about the resources you or the practice assign to various tasks. When you assign a less experienced (and presumably cheaper) resource to a task, you maximize value to the practice – experience gained and cost – but increase task risk. This maximin approach maximizes the minimum cost, but does so at increased risk.

Multiple task-solution options: Consider a task that has multiple approaches, not all of which are proven (e.g., a particular trial theory). You can minimize the maximum risk by assigning a resource who will work only in proven ways, or you can assign a creative thinker and increase the likelihood of getting an out-of-the-box solution... and increase also the likelihood of a poor solution.

Seeming to be most which we indeed least are.
William Shakespeare, *The Taming of the Shrew*

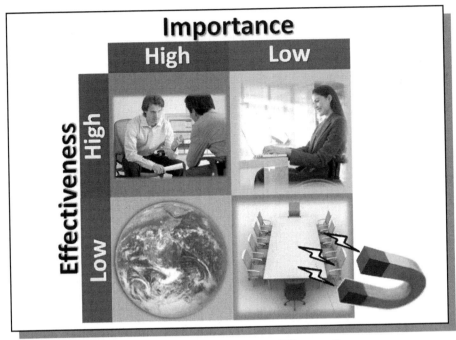

Urgent, Important, Effective

Stephen Covey, in *The 7 Habits of Highly Effective People*, pointed out how easily we mistake urgency for importance.

Urgent v. Important

Many people go overboard attacking urgent items at the expense of the truly important, especially in these always-connected, working-24/7 times. However, so many things appearing critical in the moment turn out, given time and reflection, to have been minor. The simplest solution is to unplug somewhat: check Email only a few times a day, turn off notifications on your BlackBerry, and think rather than react.

Conversely, many attorneys attach great importance to even the smallest of details. In law school, every detail was crucial. In the real world, only a limited number of items are dispositive, changing the direction of a case. You may do clients an accidental disservice by not differentiating between important and minor details; if there is a limited budget, spend it on the make-or-break items.

Important v. Effective

Even if you focus only on those items that are both important and turning points in your work, go one step further: how effectively can you *address* such items? Can you make a dent in the problem? Map your activities onto the slide's matrix; then determine how much time to invest in them.

What are some important things that you're good at? Legal work? Conferring with clients? Negotiating project details? Those areas are where you get the most leverage, the biggest bang for the buck. Project managers should target 90% of their time in this quadrant.

Every case has a bunch of not-very-important things that you can knock off quickly. Do one and you feel successful; the good news is that success in small things breeds success in larger things. Spend about 5% of your time here.

World hunger? Contributing to the practice's long-term thinking? Important, yes, even pivotal – and thus they deserve at least a little time, but don't overdo it. High-importance/low-effectiveness areas – societal or practice issues generally bigger than you are – are also worth 5% of your non-family time. Your contribution may be small, but you'll feel a lot better about yourself and your role.

That leaves a bucket of stuff that isn't terribly important... and you can't do much about. Many meetings fall into this quadrant. So do most emails, tweets, and telemarketing pitches. The goal is to spend no time in this quadrant whatsoever. You won't fully zero it out, but keep trying; this quadrant has a magnet that tries to suck all your time into it!

Things small as nothing, for request's sake only, he makes important.
William Shakespeare, *Troilus and Cressida*

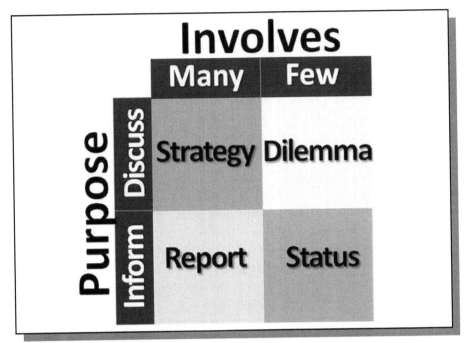

Making Meetings Productive

There is no one-size-fits-all type of meeting. There are different types of meeting, and each requires a different approach to productivity.

The Four Types of Meetings

You can classify meetings in a 2x2 matrix. On one axis is their purpose: to inform others or to discuss an issue and perhaps reach a decision. On the other axis is the size of the group of active participants (not the attendee count, but those actively engaged with the meeting's purpose).

"Strategy" meetings are the highest-value quadrant, a type of meeting mistakenly shunted aside in many guidebooks for effective meetings. These rich group discussions can be strategy and planning sessions, brainstorming, group budgeting, or resource allocation discussions.

These meetings are effective when everyone understands the purpose and the ground rules.

Reporting meetings consist of one person is informing the others in the room – a manager sharing news with her reports, a group comptroller giving a budget update. These meetings are valuable only if the news is meaningful to most of the attendees. There may be Q&A and discussion, and different people may report out during the same meeting. These meetings should be structured (see below).

Status meetings are often low in value; keep them short. Commonly an employee shares information with peers. You don't want too many of these, but brief sessions are effective at keeping the team on the same page. Consider stand-up meetings for this quadrant – where, literally, everyone is standing; it keeps the meeting short. Require agendas.

Dilemma meetings, where just a few of the participants engage in detailed problem-solving, are inefficient. Don't drag the whole group into colloquies or dilemmas. If you a meeting is turning into one of these soul-swallowing monsters, deflect it to one-on-one time.

Boosting Productivity

Meetings work best when they have:

- An agenda (for reporting and status meetings) describing items to be covered and time allotted, sent to all participants ahead of time.

- A facilitator (who may or may not be a participant) who helps the attendees stick to the agenda, but who also recognizes when value is gained by diverging from it.

- Meeting minutes – listing decisions, action items, and due dates – sent to all participants shortly after the meeting.

- Ground rules, especially for strategy meetings.

Take charge of meetings; unmanaged meetings are time wasters.

This is the very description of their meeting.
William Shakespeare, *Cymbeline*

Practical LPM

The path
is **SMOOTH**
that **LEADETH**
on to **DANGER.**

Brief #13

Checklist for Action

To make meetings more productive:

✓ *Understand the purpose of the meeting and whether few or many of the participants are central to that purpose.*

✓ *Require an advance agenda for reporting and status meetings.*

✓ *Meetings need facilitators – usually but not always the project manager. It's hard to facilitate and participate at the same time.*

✓ *Distribute meeting minutes after each meeting. Capture decisions, action items, and due dates.*

✓ *Meetings do better with explicit ground rules*

✓ *Deflect "dilemma meetings" where a few participants take up everyone's time, unless the subject is of interest to all.*

Key Takeaways

- Define a framework for project decisions that the team accepts.

- Use a RACI matrix – Responsible, Approver, Consulted, Informed – or equivalent for clarity on roles and responsibilities around decisions.

- Define a work process for intra-team communication, information sharing, reporting, tools, and so on. Use this work to build trust.

- Choose the right project management tool – if any – based on the complexity of the project and your own facility and comfort level.

- Not all project tools are schedulers.

- Map the dependencies among tasks. Sometimes one can't start until another finishes; other times, tasks need to finish at the same time.

- Once you have a work breakdown structure, task lengths, dependencies, internal deadlines such as court or filing dates, and resources, you can create a project schedule.

- Schedules can work forward from a start date or backward from a target date. (Experts at scheduling can also combine these methods.)

- The tasks on the critical path are those that, if delayed, will cause the entire project to be late.

- Fees and scope can be negotiated with the client – and with internal stakeholders. Understand the concept of marginal value, where additional work no longer delivers exceptional value.

- Don't mistake urgent for important, or important for effective.

- Meetings that "just happen" are usually unproductive; take charge.

Brief #14

Legal Project Management in Context

We could
ARRIVE
at the POINT
PROPOSED.

When you first board a fair-sized sailboat, the deck is crossed with an amazing array of ropes. (That's where we get "learning the ropes.")

Except they're not called ropes – nor are they made of hemp these days. They're known as sheets. Except the ones that go up and down. Those are halyards.

Jib sheet. Mainsheet. Cunningham. Traveler. Outhaul. Reefing lines.

Down below there's no bathroom or kitchen or beds. Instead, there's a head, a galley, berths.

If the boat has a wheel for steering, you turn it right to go right, but if it has a tiller, you push it left to go right – sorry, to starboard.

It's incredibly confusing if you only read about sailing.

But once on the boat, you can learn the basics of sailing in an afternoon. Once you feel the push of the tiller, the way the sails channel the wind and turn breeze into boatspeed, suddenly sailing starts to make sense.

You realize you don't need to know the names of all those objects. The boat may have something called a fiddle block with becket – you're likely using it to control the mainsail – but no one is asking for it by name.

Legal Project Management is like sailing; you'll learn it fastest by getting underway. The various parts may seem strange by themselves – finish-to-finish scheduling, expected risk losses, project charters. However, once you start using them, the pieces will fall into place, probably faster than the nomenclature does.

You can learn to sail in an afternoon, enough to make progress across the water in the direction you want to go.

You can do the same with Legal Project Management.

I desire no more delight than to be under sail.
William Shakespeare, *The Merchant of Venice*

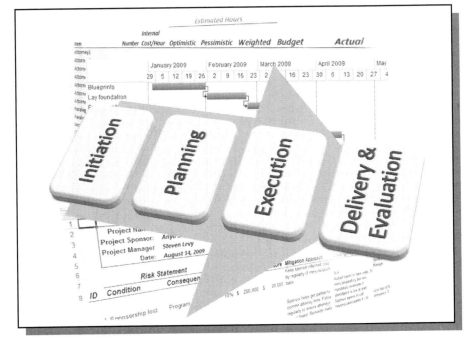

Fixed-Fee Billing and LPM

There's a book to be written on alternative billing arrangements, and this isn't it. (Richard Susskind's probably writing it right now.) However, I do want to cover the special LPM connection with fixed fees. This data also applies in house to using fixed resources to serve business clients.

Calculating Costs and Resource Needs (Pre-Agreement)

1. Before you price a bid, define the conditions of satisfaction (p. 156) and "Done" (p. 154) *in partnership with the client.*

2. Create a work breakdown structure (p. 192) to determine the necessary tasks. Assign resources – attorneys, paralegals, etc. – along with estimates of how long it will take those resources to complete the tasks. (Don't forget that project management and client communication / management are

also tasks.) Try out various combinations – e.g., an associate can do Task T in 25 hours plus 2 hours oversight for $X, while a senior attorney can do it in 15 hours for $Y.

3. Create a list of risks (p. 184) that could hurt you, and factor in their expectations of loss.

4. Consider your return on investment (p. 144) to arrive at a fee (or in-house resource load) that works for you as the core of your negotiating position. The same process should also give you the minimum fee you can charge.

Focus on "Done." Do you know what the client actually requires? Ensure all of the WBS tasks are outcome-determinative (p. 220) or required in some other way (e.g., project management).

Staying on Budget and on Track (Post-Agreement)

1. Use the pre-agreement data and Legal Project Management principles to guide the project.

2. Ensure that all resources have a very clear picture of "Done" and of the project vision. In particular, make sure they know what they *don't* need to do. Use information radiators (p. 214) to strengthen intra-team communication and sharing.

3. Implement effective change management (p. 210), decision-making guidelines (p. 244), and work processes (p. 246).

4. Follow solid Initiation, Planning, and Execution techniques, tips, and tools throughout. Keep a careful watch over actual task durations (p. 258), dependencies (p. 252), budget (p. 174), etc.

5. Contain risk by managing it effectively (pp. 184, 264).

6. Communicate based on Legal Project Management communication models (p. 216).

Thereby shall we shadow the numbers.
William Shakespeare, *Macbeth*

Responding to RFPs

Requests for proposal are the bane of business existence. I know few people who believe they work well in any business. They're disliked by sellers, buyers, and buy-side stakeholders alike; only procurement folks and consultants seem to win. However, they're a fact of life. (By the way, p. 308 has suggestions for in-house teams on creating more useful RFPs.)

What Column Are You In?

Before you respond, figure out which column you're in. Column A is the leading candidate, often having participated in writing the RFP. Column B, the challenger, has some chance of winning, but they're likely going to have to compete on the first firm's terms. Everyone else is column fodder, there to give the appearance of a broadly researched proposal.

If you're column fodder, think hard about how much time you want to devote to a bid you're unlikely to win. What concessions are you willing to make? How can you present yourself as extraordinary? Consider changing "the rules" of the RFP in a way that favors your work.

Column B needs to either beat the leader at its own game or change the game. The questions themselves in the RFP provide insight into the client's thinking, the leader's strengths, or both.

If you're the leader, your task is to defend your position.

Changing the Game

Sometimes you can change the game by responding to the RFP in a nonstandard, somewhat dramatic, memorable way. It depends on your creativity, your willingness to take a risk (remember, you're not the favorite to begin with), and the rigidity of the client's process. If the client is proceeding with a basically mathematical analysis – generally a procurement belief without much proof that it works in the legal world – you're unlikely to change that. However, if the client is truly seeking a proposal, offer yours – in whatever form makes sense to you.

Even if you fill out a 200-item detailed RFP, present along with it a two- or three-page proposal that highlights your special capabilities. Think of it as the oral argument to put a face to your written brief.

Promote Your Legal Project Management Capabilities

Play up your Legal Project Management strengths: "Our attorneys are skilled in Legal Project Management to safeguard your fiscal interests as well as your legal interests. We partner with you to determine the legal solution that best fits your business and legal needs. Then our project managers help us deliver that solution on time and on budget while maintaining great communication and controlling for unplanned events."

We could arrive at the point proposed.
William Shakespeare, *Julius Caesar*

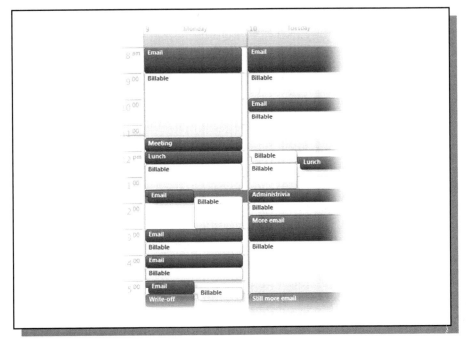

Organizing Nonbillable Time

What occupies your nonbillable or *un*-billable time (or in-house equivalents)?

- **Training and learning**, including contributing to knowledge management, adds value to the practice.

- **Business development (rainmaking)** is valuable when it succeeds.

- **Email** is surprisingly inefficient, as is Blackberry-type interruption.

- **Administrivia** adds no value. You need a minimal amount – e.g., time tracking – but you likely spend far more than the minimum.

- **Client-rejected or write-off** time is pure cost; if the client doesn't want it, don't do it. The same goes for rework.

- **Other:** from talking to kids (valuable) to checking Facebook (um...).

Accounting

If you track time, track *all* time at work. If you don't measure it, you'll have difficulty controlling it. Set up categories or clientless matters to capture each form of nonbillable time. Next, either individual attorneys or practice leadership should examine the data for patterns of waste. If practice leadership is checking, consider anonymizing the data; otherwise attorneys may be reluctant to admit to the volume of administrivia that takes time out of their days.

Recognize that attorneys who devote long hours to the office need time during the day to deal with life itself, both important family matters and the trivial (e.g., shopping on line). You'll get a better return focusing on the reduction or elimination of wasted work-related time, such as low-value meetings (p. 268).

Once you know how much time is going toward nonproductive work-related items, you can start attacking the problem. Work assiduously to minimize non-value-added activities (p. 324) as you root out rework, time waiting for others, duplication, and other waste (pp. 328, 330; "waste" is the formal name for such non-value-added tasks).

Tracking Waste When You Don't Track Hours

Even if you don't track hours, I recommend tracking everything you do for one week every three months. You'll be amazed at how much time you spend on tasks that add little value to the practice, from traveling between meetings to reacting to popup email notifications. (Keep a sheet and tick off every time you react to a popup or smartphone vibration.)

Is Legal Project Management Billable?

Legal Project Management is billable if the client says it is, of course. If you're billing hourly, you should bill project management once the case/project is underway; otherwise, include it in calculating the overall fee. Work before the project starts is a business development cost.

What, billing again?
William Shakespeare, *Troilus and Cressida*

Litigation as a Project

E-discovery has long been seen as a project, with attendant traditional-style project management. Litigation itself is also a project, or more often a series of projects.

There are benefits to seeing as separate projects each phase of lengthy litigation – pleadings and preparation, discovery and depositions, etc.:

- Some phases can be fixed fee or flat-fee books of work, while others involve some variant of hourly billing. (A flat-fee book of work would be a fixed charge for each deposition, for example.)
- Each phase might have different completion bonuses (p. 314).
- Each phase really does have separate Initiation, Planning, Execution, and Delivery/Evaluation stages.

For many aspects of litigation, you can predict the level of effort and the types of resources needed. Court calendars are set long in advance of the actual trial by most judges, offering a reasonable picture of the time until trial begins. (Unfortunately, there are some courts that exercise poor management of the workload or of the other party's continual surprise requests.) Your pretrial strategy sessions already cover much of the needed information – the number of witnesses you expect to depose, lining up experts, and so on. The number of interrogatories may vary, say, but you know on average how long it will take for these to play out.

Admittedly, e-discovery grows increasingly complex, despite such efforts as the Sedona Conference, FRCP Rules 26 and 37, and opinions by at least a few judges who have more than a token understanding of the complexity behind even simple requests. It makes sense, I think, to separate e-discovery itself into two projects, one dealing with the actual search, analysis, and production that's often largely outsourced and one with the highly variable issues outside the main flow, such as forensic analysis or extended wrangling over search terms and privilege logs.

The Tangled Web of Stakeholders

Litigation has an extremely complex group of both real and imagined stakeholders. There are the attorneys, of course. For corporate clients, the senior executive – the CEO for larger trials – is a stakeholder, as are the leaders of the business division suing or being sued. There are professionals who to some degree put their careers at stake at each trial, such as jury consultants and expert witnesses, who may want to tell you how to do your job. Each witness, each deponent also behaves like a type of stakeholder, with credibility at stake, and with both story and backstory coloring statements.

In big-ticket litigation, the project manager is probably not the lead attorney, but you can contribute immensely by helping manage the stakeholders; work toward their interests, not positions (p. 152). Use a RACI matrix to outline roles and responsibilities (p. 245) and a risk worksheet (p. 184) to manage legal as well as project risks.

What's the news with you? You told us of some suit.
William Shakespeare, *Hamlet*

The Transaction as Project

You can consider large-scale transactional work as a project: clear stages and workflow, multiple stakeholders with disparate interests, and so on. Transactions have a clear order for and timing of particular negotiations, the ongoing chess game of multiple interests expressed as positions (p. 152), and a clear map to the stages of Legal Project Management:

Initiation: What's the goal? The fallback position(s)? Who are the stakeholders? Who are the other players? (Consider the number of business-side people in an acquisition who can knock it off the rails.)

Planning: Define resources, scope, and schedule, the iron triangle (p. 172). Identify tasks and who will do them, the work breakdown structure. Mind the gaps. Get and *stay* on top of the risks – especially mitigation items around IP. Planning gets the short end of the stick all too often; don't jump over it to Execution.

Execution is much easier once you've got your ducks in a row from Initiation and Planning, especially when crunch time hits. Keep everyone informed. Utilize change management procedures to support you, not throw up barriers. Communicate.

Delivery is a signed deal – or the hard decision to walk away. **Evaluation** includes debriefing the team to get a head start on the next transaction.

Negotiation teams can have a complex structure. While there's usually a clear leader and thus a hierarchy, consider using a RACI matrix (p. 245) to clarify roles and responsibilities. Just as you often reuse clauses or even whole contracts as a starting point, use project schedules and the dependency maps they represent (p. 252) to outline the workflow and provide a roadmap for new deals.

One of the critical aspects of a large transaction is risk management. Use a risk worksheet (p. 184) to track legal or deal risks in the same way you track project risks, with mitigation and contingency plans, triggers, and easy calculation of risk exposure.

Supporting Junior Members of the Transaction Team

Transactions have a well accepted choreography, and the senior members of the team dance it skillfully from memory. The artistic director of a dance company knows he must teach new members to dance the company's works, and builds time into the troupe's schedule. A senior transaction team can do the same for their junior members using the tools of Legal Project Management.

How do you document the choreography for those new to the team? (If it sounds hard, it beats using Labanotation to record dance steps and body positions on paper.) A default work breakdown structure (p. 192) and "blank" schedule with dependencies (p. 252) cover a lot of ground to bring new team members up to speed quickly, boosting overall team efficiency.

He must not mark our contract.
William Shakespeare, *The Winter's Tale*

Legal Project Management in Context

We could
ARRIVE
at the **POINT**
PROPOSED.

Brief #14

Checklist for Action

To stick to a budget, fixed-fee or otherwise:

✓ *Use Legal Project Management for the case.*

✓ *Ensure everyone understands "Done" and the project charter – and what not to do as well as what's required.*

✓ *Use information radiators as part of a communications strategy.*

✓ *Implement change management and decision making guidelines within an agreed team work process.*

✓ *Don't shortcut Initiation or Planning to get to Execution.*

✓ *Track closely actual task durations, dependencies, and budget.*

✓ *Manage risk ferociously.*

✓ *Communicate, communicate, communicate.*

Key Takeaways

- Define conditions of satisfaction and "Done" – with the client – before pricing a bid.

- Price your bids based on the best available data, rather than on intuition, or on hope that it works out. Then factor in as needed other conditions, such as the extent to which you'll go to win the bid.

- If you're responding to an RFP, figure out which column you're in – the lead, the contender, or column fodder. Don't waste time if you're column fodder unless you can dramatically change the game.

- Organize your nonbillable hours effectively. Keep track of all time for at least a week each quarter to understand where this time is going. Avoid administrivia and other ineffective (non-value-added) uses of time.

- Time spent on Legal Project Management adds value to the client's work and is itself billable if you're tracking hours.

- Transactions themselves can be viewed as large projects.

Brief #15

Training and Coaching

I will
BELIEVE you
by the SYLLABLE
of what you shall **DELIVER**.

There are 18,000 people in the arena when the lights go down. Restless anticipation, and then a spotlight hits the stage. "Brooooooce," the crowd roars, and Bruce Springsteen – "the Boss" – takes charge.

As the band plays, he reaches out to the fans holding cardboard signs with song requests, many of them little-known tracks from albums released decades ago. He grabs some of them, the hits and the obscure. During the show, he'll hold them up, one by one, for the band, count off the beat, and the band will launch into a song they haven't played in years... or even some rock 'n' roll classic they have *never* played together.

What kind of training produces this level of musical memory and musicianship? Thirty to forty years of working as a team... and trust in "the Boss" to hold it all together if things get dicey.

You can't turn out great project managers overnight, let alone great project teams.

But the folks in Springsteen's E Street Band were experienced musicians before joining the band. They didn't have to learn how to play; they had to learn how to play *together*, and learn new songs.

Effective Legal Project Management training doesn't try to teach attorneys to become overnight project managers, a task that will (a) fail and (b) annoy the attorneys. Rather it builds on what they already know, on work they've done and lawyer habits they've acquired.

Experienced attorneys know how to play their instruments. Good training teaches them new songs. Coaching helps them play together.

Will you lead a band?
William Shakespeare, *Henry VI pt 2*

Training Delivery

There are three basic means of training participants in a Legal Project Management program: instructor-led training, electronic training, and self-study. A fourth modality, lecturing, is not well suited for project management training; it is but minimally interactive or contemplative. Factual knowledge represents a small part of what project managers must understand.

Instructor-Led ("Stand-Up") Training

Instructor-led training (ILT) will likely prove the most powerful over time because it supports all of the major training tools and techniques mentioned on the next spread. It's often called stand-up training based on the image of an instructor standing in front of a class, but good ILT belies that image with interactive and participatory leadership.

Studies have shown that for instruction-based learning, retention is equally high when the instructor is present only visually (live at a remote location). However, when ILT for Legal Project Management is delivered in person, it allows for roaming instructor participation and guidance during exercises and role-playing.

There is one significant downside to instructor-led training in the legal world: it requires not only that participants allocate time in contiguous blocks, but that the each attendee align her schedule to the *same* contiguous blocks.

Electronic Training

Electronic training, whether on the Internet or hosted on a local computer, can be effective in transmitting some Legal Project Management skills. Self-paced online training is effective at transmitting factual information and allowing trainees to explore options in case-method studies.

It is possible to add asynchronous online training – that's a fancy term for email exchanges – for exercises, for incident and case methods, and for at least some hypothetical role playing. Such online work can supplement instructor-led training or even self-study.

Self-Study

Self-study can include electronic training, self-paced learning from books such as this one (e.g., Level 3), and formal or informal on-the-job training.

Many terrific project managers have learned on the job, guided by peers and managers, self-study, and the schooling of endless mistakes. It's effective... but it's a slow process not ideally suited to the goal of helping legal professionals better manage cases.

I will believe you by the syllable of what you shall deliver.
William Shakespeare, *Pericles*

Training v. Learning

Calling the process of learning Legal Project Management "training" is partly a misnomer and partly a limitation of colloquial English; the idea of engaging, say, a "learning consultant" suggests somehow that a student has fallen behind the pace.

But effective "training" is really "learning."

It's more than a semantic distinction. It is not just a difference in perspective – i.e., mentors offer training, students pursue learning. Rather, it's push v. pull.

Training is pushing content out, offering methods, principles, answers. Learning, on the other hand, is pulling content in, absorbing those methods, principles, and answers in ways such that they enhance student capabilities.

What good trainers do is not teaching; rather, they facilitate learning.

What makes attorneys – or any professional – successful is not skills and knowledge. They are indeed required, but they are not sufficient. Rather, it's the ability to apply those skills, and to understand how and why to apply them in a fluid situation that doesn't correspond directly to a scenario they've studied.

That's why effective Legal Project Management training – or any training program that goes deeper than a single lecture or seminar – uses so many different tools, tools such as instruction, exercises, incident method and case method work, role playing, and knowledge checks. Effective business training is really defined by creating the right opportunities and environments for professionals to learn more than facts.

What Attendees Can – and Can't – Learn From Training

Participants in training will learn names for things – project stages, documents, and players. Nomenclature orders and categorizes the world they'll encounter, and it facilitates the sharing of information. They'll gain exposure to project management tools, and see new ways to use their current tools. They'll experience some common project-management scenarios, gaining at least a sense of how to manage them effectively. (Further coaching will help them map the simplified models to messy real-world encounters.) They'll learn the kinds of questions they need to ask.

They'll likely learn why project management, legal or otherwise, is harder than it looks.

They'll build a foundation for thinking and acting like project managers, a foundation on which they can build with experience.

They won't learn to be project managers from training alone.

Where learned you that?
William Shakespeare, *As You Like It*

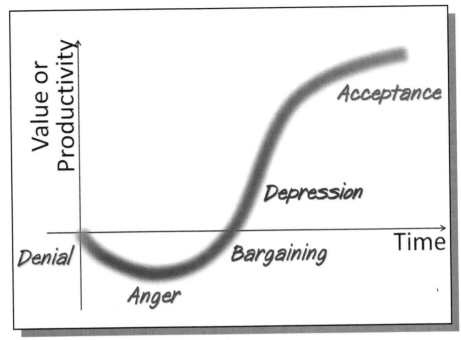

The Adoption Curve

Adopting a new way of working takes time.

The adopters generally pass through five standard stages. These stages parallel the findings of Elizabeth Kübler-Ross regarding the way we cope with grief. They apply to the introduction of almost anything new.

Denial

The first reaction to the introduction of Legal Project Management is likely to be some form of "we don't need that" or "Leonardo didn't need project management for the Mona Lisa." (Actually, he spent over four years on the painting and made minor revisions for another ten....)

Denial rapidly transforms into anger.

Anger

"Isn't my work good enough?" "I'm already trying to do the best work possible for my clients; this stuff will only make it harder."

One way to blunt the anger of this stage is to frame the problem as a pure business problem, as described as part of the Five Credos. (Credo 3, p. 28: "Participate not just in the work but in the profitability of the business" of the law firm or department.)

Bargaining

"I'll go to training only if it counts against my annual hours target" or "...if it will help with my performance review." These are accommodations you should be prepared to make, or at least to consider and negotiate.

Denial, anger, and bargaining parallel are important steps toward system change, building a "project team" and getting buy-in for the vision.

Depression

"This project management stuff takes too much time." "I'm not good at it." Applying new skills always takes time. However, this is the stage where the productivity gains finally start to outpace the time spent acquiring the skills.

Acceptance

"I feel a lot more control of the flow of my cases." "I can see a clear endpoint, which leaves me less stressed at night." This is the first stage at which you can recruit participants to evangelize the new direction, where you can secure the early wins and consolidate gains. Here is also where the deeper business value will emerge.

Adoption strives with nature.
William Shakespeare, *All's Well That Ends Well*

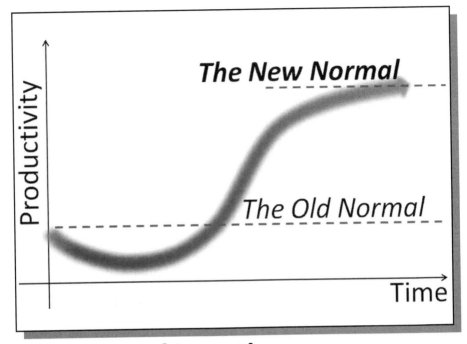

Metrics and Learning

Practices maintain their strength by learning continuously in all they do, from Continuing Legal Education to improving their tools. Enlarging on the gains of Legal Project Management likewise builds a practice's strength.

"Learning organizations" feed on continuous improvement. They define both direct metrics and – where needed – substitute metrics (p. 90) to measure their progress over time. They then drive the long-term success of an LPM program by making adjustments based on metrics, feedback, and informed observation.

Learning metrics might include the following, for example:

•   Number or percentage of attorneys trained on LPM.

- Number or percentage of attorneys using LPM after training.
- Attorney satisfaction with the LPM program.
- Client satisfaction with work performed under the guidance of Legal Project Management.

The more critical metrics, though, are those associated with the "new normal." These measurements reveal the extent to which Legal Project Management now benefits the practice.

The New Normal

Most significant changes in non-dysfunctional organizations are subject to the Kübler-Ross-derived J curve. Legal Project Management will be no exception. Early adopters will have to think through every action rather than performing automatically, which adds time and inefficiency to first steps. In addition, they'll likely make mistakes that also cost time. Proactive and on-demand coaching can mitigate but not eliminate these issues.

Shortly, though, cases on a Legal Project Management track will show significant efficiency gains. The effort will be more predictable; work will clearly relate to client value and the business bottom line; and risks will be better managed and controlled. In other words, productivity will suffer an initial dip but will soon soar above the baseline.

As the attorneys become proficient at Legal Project Management, the gains will solidify, becoming repeatable across cases and case teams. These teams will establish a new standard of productivity, the new normal.

Useful metrics measure the gap between old and new normal. Note, however, that you may not be able to establish the "old normal" baseline when you take on different kinds of work or different billing or accounting structures.

The task he undertakes is numbering.
William Shakespeare, *Richard II*

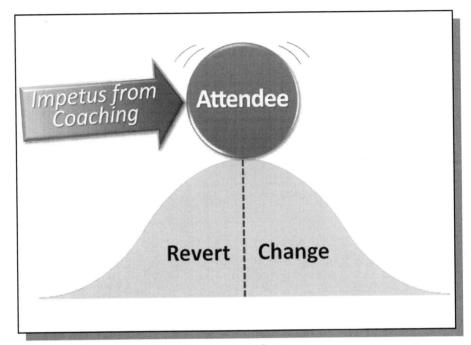

The "Why" of Coaching

Many training programs in all fields deliver suboptimal results because of insufficient follow-up. An attendee leaves the training session with good memories, positive outlooks, and perhaps some takeaway materials. She's excited to take what they've learned and put it to work.

Then the real world intrudes. There's a day worth of email needing attention. There are memos to write, meetings to attend. But eventually the attendee faces a situation that looks like a good match for the training. This is the opportunity she was waiting for.

Except that the attendee has forgotten pieces of the training. Except that under the pressure of a real-world situation she's finding it difficult to map the training to actual practice. Except that something real is at stake; safer, she thinks, to fall back on what she's done before.

Training alone is rarely sufficient when it comes to obtaining real-world results. Batting practice alone doesn't prepare a hitter to face big-league pitching, any more than law school prepares a graduating attorney for partner-level success on cases.

From the Real World

In a long corporate management career, I was able to participate in a number of very expensive four- and five-day residential training programs. Afterwards, *one* program offered *one* hour-long coaching session. Over time, most of these programs were shortened or dropped, in part because results were hard to measure. But I found telling the number of attendees who emerged from the end of each training program charged with excitement, eager to put new learning into action... and then, three to six months later, reported they had been unable to do so. Commonly, either they hadn't known how to start or had been "too busy" to try the new approaches.

Coaching would have addressed both of these blocking factors... for about the cost of each attendee's meals at these programs.

Coaching can range from training-content refreshers and reminders to specific guidance or even to partnering on a particular problem. Different situations – and different coaches – may suggest different approaches.

In general, knowledge workers who devise a solution with guidance rather than receive a one-time answer are more able to generalize their learning. They'll find it easier to rely on their own now-enhanced resources to solve future problems. Effective coaching can reinforce techniques and touchstones learned in training, helping attendees map their learning to actual problems they're currently facing.

A practice that invests in a training program can extend and protect that investment through follow-up coaching. Even more, a practice that invests in the effort needed to effect system-wide changes is committed to change; coaching helps transform that commitment into reality.

A coach doth carry thee.
William Shakespeare, *Love's Labors Lost*

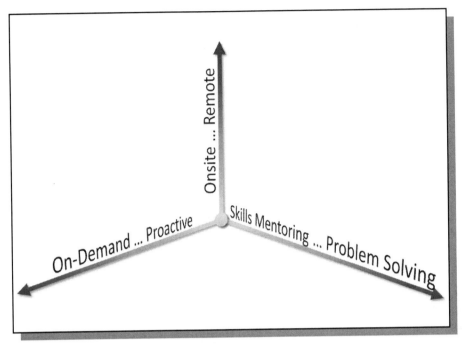

Delivering Coaching

You can think of the delivery of Legal Project Management coaching – or any business coaching – along three axes.

Proactive (Scheduled) v. On-Demand (Situational)

In proactive coaching, the employee and the coach have a prearranged coaching meeting; they may choose to define a specific topic in advance, but opportunistic coaching – the topic most pressing in the moment – is equally okay. In on-demand coaching, the employee recognizes or is told of the need for a coach, generally for a specific topic or situation, and the employee connects with the coach shortly thereafter.

Proactive coaching as a follow-up for training is an effective way to reinforce the lessons of training, to get them to "take." New practitioners of LPM benefit from consulting Legal Project Management professionals "on the fly" when questions or new situations arise, similar to the way that clients consult attorneys for situational advice.

Onsite v. Remote

Onsite coaching – especially in the employee's office, a "safe" place – can offer levels of comfort and connection hard to match otherwise. However, once the employee has a level of comfort and trust in the coach, remote coaching can prove equally valuable and effective. Remote coaching can be done via phone, via videoconference, or even via online chat or email. The last trades valuable immediacy and intimacy for time in which the participants can thoughtfully frame questions and suggestions. It also allows employee and coach to connect even when schedules are out of synch.

Skills Mentoring v. Problem Solving

Coaching can reinforce, expand on, or even re-teach skills delivered in training, in effect becoming personalized training. Coaching can also guide the employee in managing a specific problem he's wrestling with, from guided suggestions to a full problem-solving partnership.

Coaching for the Long Term

Because project management, legal or otherwise, is not a skill that can be brought to full flower overnight, you might schedule occasional ongoing proactive coaching to allow attorneys to refine their new skills or build additional skills. Providing attorneys access to coaching on demand will help them address issues as they arise, before those small issues turn into something larger.

Providing for ongoing coaching ensures that the proper time and focus are devoted to strengthening your LPM program amid the ongoing pressures of business and the practice of law. Turn short-term wins into long-term success and provide increased value to clients.

Contrive the means of meeting.
William Shakespeare, *Hamlet*

Training and Coaching

I will
BELIEVE you
by the SYLLABLE
of what you shall **DELIVER**.

Brief #15

Checklist for Action

Use metrics to track the success of training and coaching programs:

✓ *Number or percentage of attorneys trained on LPM.*

✓ *Number or percentage of attorneys using LPM after training.*

✓ *Number or percentage of attorneys utilizing coaching for guidance on specific issues.*

✓ *Attorney satisfaction with the LPM program.*

✓ *Attorney satisfaction with the training/coaching program.*

✓ *Client satisfaction with work performed under guidance of Legal Project Management.*

The last is the most important. For a firm, beware that it's a substitute metric (p. 90) for "repurchase intent," the likelihood that a client will place additional work with the firm, but it remains a vital indicator.

Key Takeaways

- It's hard to learn a practical subject such as Legal Project Management from a book alone... even (ahem!) this book.

- Use training to make these concepts come alive to attorneys.

- Good training isn't uniform or homogeneous.

- Training can be led in person by instructors or delivered electronically on line. Learners can also self-study using books such as this one.

- Adopting new practices take time. Learners pass through stages similar to the Kübler-Ross curve: denial, anger, bargaining, depression, and acceptance. Eventually the enhanced level of work becomes the "new normal."

- Supplement training with ongoing coaching. Coaching cements the gains of training as well as addressing specific issues and problems.

- Coaching is delivered along three axes:

  - Proactive (scheduled) v. on-demand (situational).

  - Onsite v. remote.

  - Skills mentoring v. problem solving.

Brief #16

The Client Perspective: Requiring LPM

They
METme
in the **DAY**
of **SUCCESS.**

Which came first, the chicken or the egg?

Which came first, firms offering Legal Project Management or clients demanding the cost certainty and schedule discipline afforded by Legal Project Management?

Firms are beginning to look seriously at Legal Project Management, and some are embracing it, recognizing the increased value it brings them. They also see it as a way to better serve demanding clients in an age when those clients no longer accept "for services rendered" billing or offer a blank check for near-unlimited hours.

Clients waiting passively for firms to adopt LPM-style fiscal, schedule, and outcome discipline are missing a bet, as are those who would deal only with firms already aboard. Clients can take the lead here, encouraging their firms to adopt the principles of project management in order to work better together.

More than just talk up LPM, clients can structure their work such that Legal Project Management is a natural firm response. They can present both individual matters and an *approach* to managing matters that leads their firms to concentrate on outcomes ("Done") rather than on effort, to engage in detailed planning and risk management, and work to meet the client's *business* objectives by handling the client's legal needs.

Many clients already have project management structures, often in the form of a project management office (PMO). While I believe it would be a mistake to give over client-side Legal Project Management to a group without deep sensitivities to the way the legal world is different, there is nevertheless a lot to learn from these internal organizations.

Which came first? Neither the chicken nor the egg cares which came first; they just focus on the process. From the egg's standpoint, a chicken is just an egg's way of making another egg.

Mine honest friend, will you take eggs for money?
William Shakespeare, *The Winter's Tale*

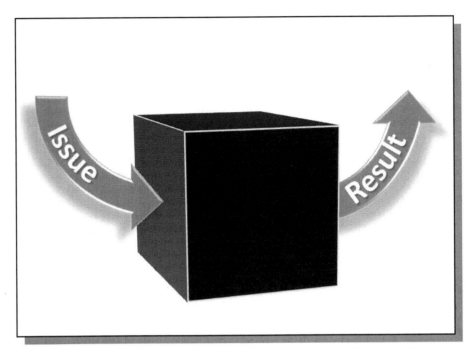

LPM and the Changing Law Practice

Clients today worry about the costs of legal services; about the lack of cost certainty, knowing in advance what a particular legal project will cost; about the number of associates billing in excess of their relative value; about being nickel-and-dimed on bills; about putting their legal work through a "black box" into which they cannot peer.

Clients unhappy with the current state of law practice might seek the culprit in the mirror.

It's a hard truth, but clients have allowed undesired behavior to take root and grow to full flower. If you don't ask how much it costs, or better yet tell the practice how much time or money you think a matter is worth, then why shouldn't they spend freely in pursuing every thread, checking every possibility in support of their obligation to you? If you negotiate only rates, then the conversation is solely about money, not efficacy or value.

Thus the smart in-house legal departments are looking to Legal Project Management. Via Legal Project Management, they can take a new approach to the business of law and the means by which they manage its time, money, and delivered value. As an arm of a corporate enterprise, in-house legal is a business that is subject to business budgets and business economics.

Client-Side Options and Approaches

Legal Project Management is not synonymous with fixed-fee or other alternative fee arrangements; firms who manage cases with project-management acumen and discipline can deliver more value in fewer hours. Legal Project Management helps you establish both the matter's goals and a working arrangement that will benefit both the firm and the client.

As a client, you can choose between selecting firms that have a Legal Project Management competency or nudge your existing firms into developing such a competency. Given the number of firms and matters for in-house departments, it's not an either/or choice; you can send some matters to new firms while urging one or more of your principal firms to use LPM to manage the matters you place with them. Sometimes the knowledge of new and valid competition for various types of matters will spur all involved, new firms and old, to deliver more cost-effective results.

Departments can use LPM-focused RFPs and quality metrics to guide their firms' approach to delivering the specific value they need. They may choose to learn the techniques of Legal Project Management to become better administrators and managers of their firm-based legal work. They can even implement Legal Project Management themselves – for their own work, to better organize and supervise outside work, or both.

I have been in continual practice.
William Shakespeare, *Hamlet*

What Can You Reasonably Expect?

Consider the question for a minute as customer/vendor rather than client/firm. What do you expect of your vendors?

- **Good value** at a quality level appropriate to the price paid. As a shopper yourself, you have different expectations for Neiman-Marcus and Wal-Mart, for Lexus and Kia; each serves its own target market.

- **Responsiveness** to your needs, questions, and issues. You expect vendors to deliver what you need, not what they want to sell you.

- **Compliance** with your standards and methods. You would expect an office furniture vendor to invoice you properly and at the agreed price, deliver on schedule, and be up front about unavoidable issues.

You should expect and demand the same of your legal suppliers.

It's reasonable to require them to use Legal Project Management techniques to manage your legal work. They needn't be the specific techniques of this book, but it's appropriate to require them to show how they'll keep costs under control, minimize the impact of unplanned events (risks, p. 184), and deliver the specific work you need on schedule.

It's also reasonable to require data corresponding to the metrics you're using (p. 310), with some negotiation on which metrics are both useful and easily obtained. Many corporate departments, for example, track "shadow hours" on bills even in fixed-fee matters (see below).

Finally, it's reasonable to expect the firm to deliver what you and they agreed on, absent major surprises neither of you could foresee.

Tracking Firm Costs

Why should you care about firm costs on, say, a fixed-fee matter? First, the client/firm relationship is also a collegial partnership, with or without Legal Project Management; you need your firms to be fiscally responsible so they can keep employing great attorneys on whose work you'll rely. Second, a demonstrated ability to manage costs translates into an ability to manage other, outcome-determinative aspects of the project. Third, watching how much effort a firm is putting into certain aspects of complex cases is often an early indicator that you and the firm aren't aligned on some aspect of the case, such as the depth to which to pursue a particular question (p. 173). Finally, there are unknowns in most projects, legal and otherwise, that should be shared risks; you may not want your firm cutting corners on critical work in the event of a surprise neither of you anticipated, just so they can meet the budget.

Jeffrey Carr, GC of FMC, views value-based fees as transformational: Fixed fee (p. 312), budgets with implications (p. 315), risk sharing, efficiency expectations (p. 311). I think that's a valuable separation from hourly billing – which remains pay-for-time, not transformational or value-based, even if rates are discounted, blended, or frozen.

What shalt thou expect?
William Shakespeare, *Cymbeline*

Creating Useful RFPs

Traditional requests for proposal (RFPs) tend toward laundry lists of "must have" and "should be." The problem is exacerbated when multiple people, each with a slightly different agenda, add their own items to the RFP. Sometimes the progenitors add a complex, pseudo-mathematical scoring system that muddles more than clarifies the outcome.

There is a better way.

Specify "Done": In effect, create a model project charter (p. 158) with a clear "Done" statement (p. 154). "Here is what the completed matter will look like; now explain how you'll get here, when, and for how much." Include clear background on your environment – your level of involvement in managing the matter, the business client's availability and involvement, and even your conditions of satisfaction (p. 157).

Avoid "column fodder": If you expect to use Firm F but corporate policy requires an RFP, you're shortchanging either your employer or the can't-win firms that keep the pretense of an open, competitive process. Don't work around the open-bidding issue by allowing a preselected vendor to write the RFP unless that firm will be the sole bidder; otherwise, this practice does a disservice to competing firms and to your corporation. Do an honest RFP and be open to better alternatives.

You may find that an honest, open evaluation challenges your originally preferred firm to create a better solution for you than they otherwise might have done.

Don't let a bidding firm write it: Doing so in a competitive situation gives that bidder an advantage because the RFP will fit best with what that firm can deliver. If you're not sure what services you need, invite firms to present their own proposals rather than respond to yours.

Allow counterproposals: Don't get locked into your own format. Firms hire some very smart people; you want that intelligence representing you. Be open to their suggestions on approaches to your issues. Perhaps they've done similar work and can draw on their experience.

Don't attach mathematical values to non-quantifiable items: It's pseudo-science to mathematically weight answers to items such as experience or quality. If two firms are so close you think you need a spreadsheet to make a choice, step back and look over the proposals anew. What resonates with you? What one item matters most? If you think it's still a tie, flip a coin; when the coin's in the air, you'll know which way you're hoping it comes down!

Keep it short: Limit the "meat" items to a handful, less than a page. People can effectively juggle about seven items simultaneously; consider limiting your true evaluation questions to seven or so items. Put separate "qualification" items on other pages if you need them – e.g., availability, deadlines, number of practitioners in a given specialty.

In sequel, all, according to their firm, proposed.
William Shakespeare, *Henry V*

Directing Firms Via Metrics

It's a management maxim: You get what you measure.

What are you measuring from your firms today? What results do you want? What might you measure instead?

Providing Misleading Incentives

If you measure cost per hour – hourly rates – you'll get lower rates... but not necessarily lower costs. Attorneys try to be ethical; nonetheless, you're providing a strong incentive to bill extra, not-really-needed hours to maintain firm profits. In addition, if a firm can get $500/hour for a senior attorney from one client but only $400/hour from another for the same attorney, the firm has an incentive to move that attorney to the higher-paying work.

If you measure cost per matter, you're making strides, but you accidentally provide an incentive to do less than great work, to work quickly with less expensive resources. Sometimes, this approach can actually work in your favor; I've known clients to spend two or three times what a matter is worth because they failed to offer clear direction; measuring cost per matter would have helped quite a bit.

Output (Results-Based) Metrics

Both cost-per-hour and total cost are input metrics (p. 84); tie results to metrics via output metrics, using Legal Project Management tools.

Done: All projects should have a "Done" statement (p. 154), though not always by that name. Whether called "Done," critical-to-quality (CTQ) factors, completion criteria, or Tommie, this expression of the desired result should be a primary metric for measuring firms. "Done" may not be always measurable on a numerical scale, such as "file 18 patents by end of year" but a good "Done" statement has clearly stated pass/fail criteria wherever a numerical model doesn't make sense.

Conditions of satisfaction (p. 157) can be negotiated between client and firm; these too, like "Done," make for good output metrics.

Cost should remain a factor, of course – just not the only factor. As part of this metric, consider firm efficiency, which is what most of this book is focused on. Consider efficiency bonuses (p. 315) to help drive firm efficiency, which translates into client value.

Schedule is a good metric when the firm is in control of the schedule; however, it's a bad idea when the *client* has a major role delivering material to the firm. Your lateness should not penalize the firm. Also, be aware that small delays on your part can have big impacts on the schedule, such as the roofer delay at the bottom of p. 255.

See p. 314 for a discussion of incentives as output metrics.

Tell me for truth the measure.
William Shakespeare, *Henry VI pt 3*

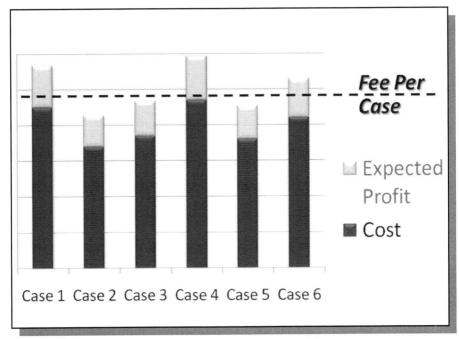

Instituting Fixed-Fee Billing

Many firms aren't yet comfortable with fixed-fee billing on other than the most repetitive matters, such as patent prosecution or immigration applications. They worry that they'll overrun their estimates and lose money.

For a firm that doesn't implement Legal Project Management, it's a legitimate fear. Even for a firm well versed in Legal Project Management, overruns remain a worry if the firm lacks sufficient prior data from which to draw good estimates.

It's also troubling to a firm if they don't have a preexisting relationship with a client. A spate of revisions and change orders (p. 210) can strain the relationship and/or destroy their fair profit.

The Shadow Bill

Some in-house departments have mitigated these fears by asking for "shadow bills," an hourly accounting delivered in addition to the fixed-fee (or other alternative-fee) bills. The firms submit shadow bills through the normal (electronic) invoice process either flagged as "do not pay" or with hourly costs marked as $0.

Such an arrangement for the first few matters allows the firm and client to easily negotiate an additional charge when extraordinary circumstances cause a matter to cost more than forecast. It also gives the firm and the client the opportunity to review the work monthly to determine together how the actual work is aligning with estimates. It's an opportunity for the client to say, "You're going too deep on this minor aspect," or for the firm to ask, "Are we attacking this issue as you expected?"

On Average

The firm should be able to make a fair profit "on average" across a book of work. Particular cases may run a bit more or less than expected, but spreading the vagaries across half a dozen cases usually causes them to even out.

Averages aren't perfect, though. If your head is encased in ice and you stand in a pot of boiling water, *on average* you're at a reasonable temperature. Averages are thrown off by outliers, instances outside of the expected range. To put it another way, Bill Gates and I have an *average* net worth of billions of dollars... but the money's mostly on Bill's side.

I recommend that you handle outliers – significant unexpected events the firm couldn't have foreseen – as exception cases and arrange to renegotiate them separately. Your goal is to get more cost-effective service and higher value, not force the firm to absorb your risks.

Make me a fixed figure.
William Shakespeare, *Othello*

Completion and Success Bonuses

Most corporate managers are paid on a mixed model, a base salary plus a bonus contingent on performance against objectives set the previous year.

In effect, they're paid a success bonus.

The extreme success bonus in the legal world is the contingent fee arrangement. Not all legal work is amenable to contingent fees, nor are they necessarily appropriate for most corporate work. However, if you remove the contingency connotation, the agreed-fee-plus-bonus arrangement is a powerful incentive to do good work efficiently, a "budget with implications" in Jeff Carr's (FMC) terminology.

You get what you measure, and money is a powerful measuring stick.

Early Completion Bonus and Hourly Billing

Firms often fear that finishing early in hourly work – fewer hours than planned – will cost them. As noted on p. 310, hourly work offers misleading incentives. You can correct for this effect by offering a bonus for early completion. This bonus, often stated as a percentage of the savings, is a true win-win situation. The client saves money vis-à-vis the estimate, and the extra money for the firm is pure profit (i.e., has effectively zero cost associated with earning it).

Early-completion bonuses can also be used in fixed-fee work, especially when there is a third party involved. The firm's strong Legal Project Management skills generally result in reasonable estimates for their own work. You can still provide an incentive for, say, bringing another party early to the negotiating table or avoiding a protracted e-discovery period that runs up costs without necessarily altering the outcome.

Success or Mission Bonus

For matters whose outcome is truly in doubt – litigation or acquisitions, for example – consider using an incentive bonus for success on the merits. When these matters get to crunch time, give the firm a financial incentive, in addition to their own pride, to use their strongest resources. Use a variant of the "Done" statement or project vision (p. 160) to define success beyond a baseline.

Other Bonuses

A **staffing bonus** is an incentive to the firm to staff a key section of a project with a specific high-powered, highly effective attorney.

A **knowledge transfer** bonus encourages the firm to share their work product with other firms you may hire for similar matters. You can force the issue as work for hire, but a small bonus might be more effective.

Efficiency bonuses can include any combination of these methods.

They met me in the day of success.
William Shakespeare, *Macbeth*

The Client Perspective: Requiring LPM

They
METme
in the **DAY**
of **SUCCESS**.

Brief #16

Checklist for Action

In creating an RFP for a legal project, consider these characteristics:

✓ *Specify "Done" and the deliverables of the project charter.*

✓ *Don't throw in a bunch of firms as column fodder just to meet corporate guidelines; keep the process open and fair in order to get the best results.*

✓ *If you intend to have only one bidder, do so straightforwardly.*

✓ *Don't let a bidder write or co-write a competitive RFP.*

✓ *Allow counterproposals from the firms. The goal is to get to the best result, not check the box in a corporate process.*

✓ *Don't use pseudo-science or pseudo-math to rate non-mathematical items.*

✓ *Keep it short; seven "meat" items is a good target.*

Key Takeaways

- Legal Project Management is not synonymous with fixed-fee billing, though it provides a support structure for effective fixed-fee billing that benefits both firm and client.

- No matter what the billing arrangement, high level expectations shouldn't change: good value at an appropriate level of quality and depth, responsiveness to client needs, and compliance with client standards and methods.

- Requests for proposal (RFPs) are widely used – and misused – in obtaining bids from suppliers. They're now making their way into the legal world.

- Use output (results) metrics to encourage firms to deliver the results you seek. Useful metrics relate to the project vision and "Done," the conditions of satisfaction, schedule (to the extent the firm is in control of it), and cost. Note that cost is not first among equals on the list.

- Consider "shadow bills" to ease firms – and yourself – into the world of fixed-fee billing.

- Firms don't want to absorb the cost of client uncertainty; negotiate agreements that cover the firms in case of significant events they couldn't have predicted.

- Use bonuses to align firm incentives with your own. Early completion bonuses benefit both firm and client, as do success bonuses.

Brief #17

Lean Six Sigma in 30 Minutes: A Roadmap to Value

Set
the **NEEDLESS**
PROCESS
BY.

My initial Six Sigma training lasted a bit longer than 30 minutes.

Some of that time was spent on exercises cementing the concepts or helping us apply them to our own departments. Some time went to examples highlighting or clarifying aspects of the methodology. A fair amount was devoted to the mathematics and statistical analyses that are part of a full Six Sigma regimen. There was Q&A, self-study, small-group learning, and so on, even a bit of process-improvement history.

The section that drove it home took a bit less than 30 minutes. We whittled down a process until only the necessary pieces were left. We then examined what they had in common.

The effect of each critical task was visible to the customer. More than just visible, each required component was something that the client or customer wanted or needed, something that clearly – from the *client's* standpoint – added value to the delivery. And in order to add value, the process had to change the work, had to actually modify the output, the item being delivered.

The things that people did for or to each other, invisible to the customer inside the black box of the practice, did not transfer value to the customer. No matter how much those things meant to the people working on them, if they didn't affect the output in a way visible and meaningful to the customer, their value was tenuous at best.

I realized how much work – "waste" – we could strip away.

I don't mean to trivialize Six Sigma by suggesting you can learn it in 30 minutes and a dozen pages. You can't. But I hope in 30 minutes I can help you understand why Lean Six Sigma in particular has made such in difference in so many different situations. I hope I can show *you* value, and help you determine whether it might be able to boost your practice.

Long time have I watched. Watching breeds leanness.
William Shakespeare, *Richard II*

What Is Six Sigma?

Six Sigma is a manufacturing business approach to improving overall results by reducing the defect rate. A defect originally meant a manufacturing defect, but it now refers to anything that reduces the quality of the output. A legal defect, for example, could include an error in a pleading, but it also could be a billed item not paid by the client or even an unproductive internal meeting.

"Six sigma" literally refers to the statistical term "standard deviation," represented by σ, sigma. An event six standard deviations from the mean, six sigmas away, will occur, in theory, only 3.4 times in 1,000,000 chances.

Because of its manufacturing history, Six Sigma is often couched in complex mathematics, which makes sense when you're stamping out millions of widgets. It also borrows from the martial arts, with novice practitioners being called "green belts" who can progress to "black belt" and even "master black belt" status.

Cut through the mysticism and math to find some very fine ideas applicable to the practice and project management of law:

- Make your processes predictable and repeatable.

- Changes require measurable results expressed in terms of financial return. Advocates say, "You can't change what you can't measure."

- Use good metrics to ensure any movement is in the right direction.

- Use data, not intuition, as the foundation for decision-making.

- Change is a process: DMAIC = Define, Measure, Analyze, Improve, Control (i.e., maintain, but that would have given a two-M acronym).

What Is Lean?

Lean manufacturing is an approach to product quality championed codified by Toyota founder Sakichi Toyoda. Based on the work of W. Edwards Deming, it was originally called the Toyota Production System.

Now called Lean or Lean Manufacturing, it is less mathematical than Six Sigma, and I consider it more easily mated to non-industrial applications. Many quality leaders have combined the best features of Lean and Six Sigma – both are based on Deming's work – and called the result Lean Six Sigma, including the intended pun on Six Sigma's very un-lean mathematical and process models.

Lean Six Sigma fits well with Legal Project Management.

This brief offers a series of short tutorial spreads on four of the key concepts, in the context of legal work and Legal Project Management. These concepts codify ideas that are for the most part intuitive and probably familiar.

What is six?
William Shakespeare, *Richard II*

Root Cause Analysis

Root cause analysis is a systematic attempt to discover the factors that affect a process, procedure, or event. There are usually multiple factors that combine to produce a result. Rarely is it the superficial manifestation of those factors that truly causes the result – which means that if you change only those superficial factors, you're probably not fixing the underlying problem.

For example, if my tire goes flat, changing the tire "fixes" the problem only to the extent that I can keep driving. Should I assume my tire went flat because it I ran over an unseen nail in the road? It's possible my parking style – scraping the curb to be sure I was close – abraded the sidewall, or perhaps I kept it chronically underinflated and wore down the tread prematurely. The latter are fixable "driving-process" problems.

The Process of Root Cause Analysis

Locate the root cause(s) via investigation, evidence/data, and analysis. Test your hypotheses if you can. Try to address the root rather than intermediate causes; that's not always possible, but working as far down the root as you can minimizes recurrence of related problems.

The numerous formal processes for performing root cause analysis all follow similar steps:

1. Define the problem.

2. Gather evidence – measurable data if possible.

3. Identify causal relationships, moving down the roots.

4. Identify which causes you can actually change.

5. Identify practical, practicable solutions that prevent recurrence without causing other problems.

6. Implement, observe, and measure your changes.

Techniques for Root Cause Analysis

There are numerous techniques available. They fall into categories:

- Fault-tree analysis, building up a tree of cause-and-effect, e.g., Six Sigma's fishbone diagram, resembling the roots in the slide at left.

- Waste (p. 328) or barrier analysis, finding impediments to the easy flow of processes.

- Depth questioning, such as the Five Whys (p. 324).

- Change analysis, examining recent changes to see their *real* effects.

In a group of causes, a very few of them will have the largest effect – called the 80/20 or Pareto rule. Those are the root causes to attack.

The true cause, the false way.
William Shakespeare, *Henry IV pt 2*

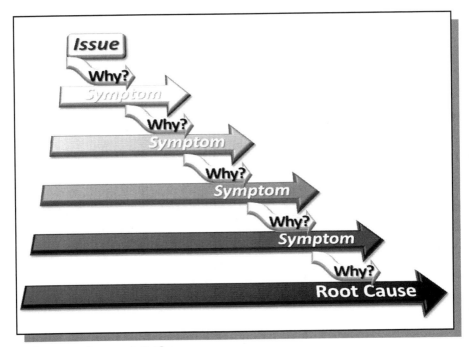

The Five Whys

Sakichi Toyoda of Toyota Motors is credited with inventing a technique called "the Five Whys." Simply stated, you keep asking "Why?" until you get to the root of the problem.

The Five Whys isn't foolproof. It's easy to stop at a symptom rather than getting to the root cause. It's even easier to be totally annoying if you enable your inner three-year-old; make sure those you're questioning understand what you are doing. They must be full participants in problem-solving. There must be 50 ways to ask the necessary questions, most without using the word "why."

Different questioners may elicit different answers; different people may supply different answers even to a consistent questioner. Nor is the right number always five. But it's almost never one... or none.

Characteristics of a Five Whys Root Cause

Action-oriented: The cause suggests a course of action, as in the example below – whether or not you are in a position to carry out that action.

Non-symptomatic: Some factor distinguishes the cause from the symptoms uncovered by the preceding Whys. A Why producing a complete new direction suggests that the preceding Why is a root cause.

Finding a root cause doesn't imply that you're ready or able to address it. What's the root cause of The Beatles breaking up? (Oh, come on, Yoko was a *symptom*. In reality, there was likely no way at the time to solve the band's problems and keep the lads together.)

Example: The Five Whys and the Golf Swing

A golfer complains that he doesn't hit the ball as far as he should.

---

1. Why don't you hit it far enough? *I don't generate sufficient clubhead speed.*

2. Why don't you generate more speed? *I use my arms rather than my body to power my swing.*

3. Why don't you use your body more? *I've never learned how.*

4. Why haven't you learned? *I've never taken lessons.*

5. Why haven't you taken lessons? *I'm too embarrassed to ask for help.*

We now have a useful cause that is action-oriented (take some lessons!) and isn't a symptom. Note that further questioning will wander off into psychology, the new direction noted above.

Use the Five Whys as a tool to get at the cause of problems on your project. It also works for dissecting hardened positions (p. 152).

You will demand of me why I do this?
William Shakespeare, *Measure for Measure*

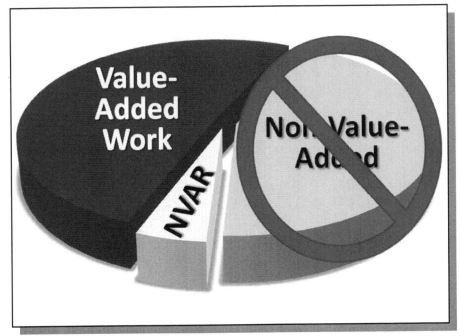

Non-Value-Added (NVA) Activity

In Lean Six Sigma, activity is considered valuable when:

1. It changes the "work" – the output or deliverable – ...

2. ...in a way that is visible to the client/customer...

3. ...and is desired by the client/customer.

Any activity that does not fulfill all criteria is NVA, non-value-added.

"Visible" doesn't literally mean "by sense of sight," nor must it be immediately visible. For example, adding insulation to the attic when building a house isn't visible to most homeowners, but its effects are noticeable in the winter. Likewise, the value of 50-year roof shingles over 20-year shingles is felt only over time (or in big windstorms).

These two additions represent added value to *most* buyers. Consider, however, a buyer in temperate San Diego who wants to build inexpensively but plans to upgrade later. How long will it take for *extra* insulation to earn back its costs? What's the value of 50-year shingles if she plans to install a metal or tile roof in a decade?

Test all of the work you do against the three requirements for value. Internal status reports. Too many practice meetings. Filling out forms to use Westlaw. Pre-bill internal reviews. (Get it right the first time.) Travel when high-definition videoconferencing would suffice. Doing more work than the client requested or needs (p. 173). Lengthy real-time emails with the attorney in the next office. NVA, NVA, NVA. One of the easiest savings in a practice – and on a project – is to eliminate the waste (p. 328) from non-value-added activity. It adds up. It costs you.

Even when you're billing or charging back hourly, any work the client doesn't want to pay for is NVA. At $250/hour, saving even 15 minutes a day on eliminated NVA could allow an attorney to bill an additional $15,600. Eliminate as much as you can; participate in practice profitability and increase client satisfaction. On a project, use the Legal Project Management concepts of a clear vision and task management to minimize tendencies toward NVA activity.

NVAR: Non-Value-Added but Required

Sometimes you must do work classified as NVA by the criteria above, such as keeping track of time for hourly billing. Such work is NVAR, non-value-added but required. You could also think of it as work with the practice as the client; however, approaching client-related work with the practice as the target removes the client as the focus of the attorney's efforts.

There is some work for which the client truly *is* the practice, where there is no external client in the picture. Examples include continuing legal education and business development. Even in these cases, rigorously apply the three criteria on the facing page.

Thou wilt but add increase.
William Shakespeare, *Henry VI pt 2*

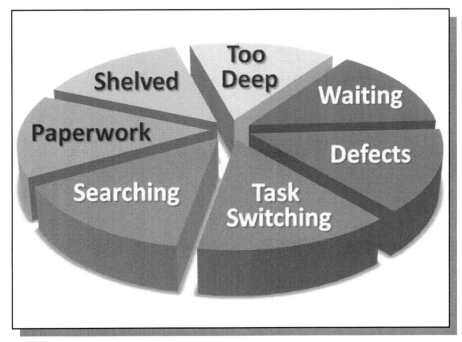

The Seven Wastes

Here are Toyoda's seven wastes mapped to Legal Project Management:

Toyota Production System	Legal Project Management
Excess inventory	Work started and then put aside
Extra processing	Extra processes and paperwork. Includes duplicate communication, telling multiple team members information previously shared (*NVA*)
Overproduction	Doing more (deeper) work than necessary for the client (p. 173, *NVA*)

Transportation (moving of product that doesn't add value)	Task or context switching (p. 330; *NVA*)
Motion (people or equipment moving without adding value)	Tracking down people with answers (lack of a knowledge management system; *NVA*)
Waiting (the product sits waiting to be worked on, leading to extra inventory)	Waiting, being unable to work on a task while waiting for a resource to become available or for another task to complete
Defects	Defects – work of lower quality than the client expected

Note that four of these seven legal project wastes are non-value-added activity (p. 326) and thus should be easy to spot; attorneys are usually aware of when they're doing work that adds little or no value.

Attacking Waste

That four of the seven legal project wastes are NVA doesn't mean the fixes are easy; implementing and getting people to use a knowledge management system is quite hard, for example. However, overproduction (depth) and transportation (context switching) should be on your hit-list per the referenced pages in this book.

You're undoubtedly already tracking down defects, substandard work. Attack the waiting problem with effective Legal Project Management to properly schedule tasks (p. 252). Keeping the team in synch with the project charter (p. 158), accurate task lists (p. 192), and information radiators (p. 214) will minimize or eliminate work that is later discovered to be off target after time has been spent on it.

Attack waste relentlessly. The money you save may be your own.

The clock upbraids me with the waste of time.
William Shakespeare, *Twelfth Night*

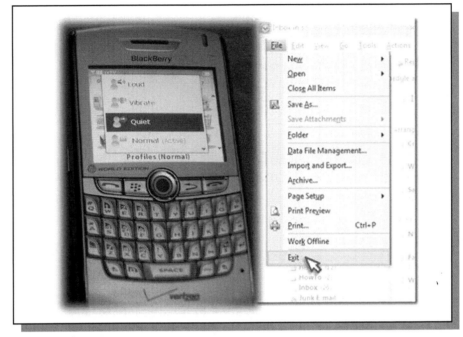

Email-Related Waste

Email inefficiency and its relative, smartphone (e.g., BlackBerry) distraction, deserve their own Lean Six Sigma place in heck.

Much is deservedly made of work/life balance, but a significant source of waste is misaligned work/*work* balance. Common misalignments include mistaking urgent for important (p. 266) and unproductive meetings (p. 268). The biggest imbalance is so ubiquitous it's become almost invisible.

What would you pay for software that gives you back 30 minutes a day? That's 2.5 hours/week. 130 hours – three full weeks – each year. What would you pay for three extra weeks of vacation? Granted, you have to take those weeks 30 minutes at a time, but still, getting home to your loved ones 30 minutes earlier? Sleeping in 30 minutes later? Doing 30 minutes more of productive and billable work?

What if I told you it took only three clicks? Now how much would you pay? But wait, there's more! This tool can actually improve your concentration and make you more productive. *Now* how much would you pay? Okay, enough channeling Ed Valenti. (You know who he is if you recognize the line, "The hand can be used like a knife, but this method doesn't work with a tomato.")

Focus, Focus, Focus

Concentration is precious. Whenever mental tasks are interrupted, it takes measurable time to recover, to rebuild whatever mental models and structures we've been contemplating. Eric Horvitz's studies suggest that recovery from an interruption averages 15-30 minutes. Per interruption.

Cut down on interruptions, and you get 15, 30, even 60 minutes a day back. Closing your door, if you have one, is one strategy, though the separation as a project manager from your team is not necessarily positive. However, the biggest time savings comes from three clicks or a few button presses.

Close email. Leave it off for at least two hours, then check it *briefly*. Lather, rinse, repeat. Set your smartphone or BlackBerry so that it *doesn't vibrate* (or beep) when you receive new messages. Check it likewise only every few hours. Set aside time for these tasks; in fact, make them real tasks with allotted time. Some people even block out these times on their calendars.

The world won't end if you don't respond instantly to email. It won't even pass you by. Clients won't disappear; they have your phone number, and a two- or three-hour response time is reasonable, as long as a) the rest of your client communication is solid (p. 164) and b) you let your clients know that a few hours is your standard response time – and you tell them why. They'll understand that you are committed to doing the best work possible, which requires focus, and that your focus benefits *them*.

He hath not failed to pester us with message.
William Shakespeare, *Hamlet*

Improve Processes: Remove Waste

There are three wide roads to process improvement via waste reduction.

Get Rid of Needless Processes

Processes add value only to the extent they change your output in a way visible to and desired by the client. If the client doesn't need or value it, you shouldn't be billing for it... so perhaps you shouldn't do it.

For example, how often do you review contracts generated automatically? Clearly, a small number of reviews are needed as part of auditing your software solution – i.e., with the *practice* as client – but at what point are you duplicating work? Are there unnecessary processes related to billing? To hiring associates or other employees?

Eliminate Over-Resourced Work

A few years ago, a client looking over a firm's bill spotted a partner doing an associate-level task but billing partner rates. Apparently the attorney had begun doing it many years ago... and kept doing it while progressing through the firm's ranks. From the client's standpoint, that's waste – and it caused the client to shift work away from the firm.

On a fixed-fee case, over-resourcing work will significantly eat into firm effectiveness; it's waste. Sometimes it may be necessary to meet a tight deadline (p. 212), but do so fully aware of the cost consequences.

Streamline Existing Processes

A few years ago, the Great Ormond Street Hospital for Children brought in the Ferrari racing team to improve their processes. The hospital thought they were doing quite well; they were clearly saving young lives at risk. Yet by working with the racing-team pit crew they recognized their processes, though seemingly effective, were inefficient, disordered, and duplicative.

Lean Six Sigma recommends a five-step process for removing waste from processes, called DMAIC (pronounced duh-MAY-ick).

- Define project goals and map the current process.

- Measure the current process using direct rather than substitute metrics (p. 90) to the extent possible.

- Analyze both the measurements and the process itself, using the Five Whys (p. 324), root cause analysis (p. 322), and so on.

- Improve the process based on the steps above.

- Control and maintain the process, measuring your gains and being alert for "relapses."

Set the needless process by.
William Shakespeare, *Measure for Measure*

Lean Six Sigma in 30 Minutes: A Roadmap

Set
the **NEEDLESS**
PROCESS
BY.

Brief #17

Checklist for Action

To eliminate work that doesn't add value to either the practice or the client, concentrate on the seven wastes:

✓ Work started and then put aside.

✓ Extra processes and paperwork, including duplicate communication.

✓ Doing more (deeper) work than necessary for the client.

✓ Task or context switching – e.g., too much attention to email.

✓ Tracking down people with answers.

✓ Waiting on a task to become "ripe."

✓ Defects, work of lower quality than the client expected.

Key Takeaways

- Lean Six Sigma is an approach to reducing process overhead focusing on removing non-value-added activity – waste – from processes.
- Use root cause analysis to dig deep into inefficiency with techniques such as
  o Fault-tree analysis such as fishbone diagrams;
  o Waste analysis, rooting out process waste;
  o Depth questioning, such as the Five Whys;
  o Change analysis.
- Use the Five Whys to break through facile answers and work toward that actual, fixable cause of waste-related problems.
- Value-added activity changes the output in a way that is visible to and desired or needed by the customer. Anything else is non-value-added (NVA) activity.
- Some NVA activity may prove to by NVAR, non-value-added but required, but strive to minimize NVAR as well as pure NVA.
- Understand and eliminate the seven wastes.
- Shut down email and turn off BlackBerry notifications. Check them on a regular but occasional basis – say, every couple of hours. Interruptions to your thought processes cost more than you can gain from instant notification of messages – most of which don't require replies in any case.
- Examine your processes for those where you can reduce the amount of processing and those you can eliminate entirely.
- Watch for work being performed by overly expensive (relative to the work involved) resources.

AT THE END

AFTERMATH

Some concluding words.

And then a few lists.

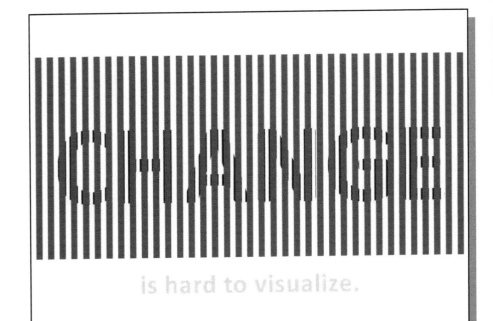

is hard to visualize.

Afterword

Change is hard – hard to visualize, hard to effect, hard to accept.

But change will come; that's not in question. The question is this: will you be out in front of that change, or will you chase it? Will you take the lead, winning new success for your practice, or will you wait for others?

Behind the Curve

Some are threatened by change – by the act of change itself, or by the way it will affect the way they work. Who might be threatened? An attorney used to working without constraints. One who sees herself as an artisan of a medieval guild, possessor of arcane secrets. One who bills numerous hours for their own sake, whether or not they represent the best value for the client.

The **active resistors** will let you know who they are. You can deal with them straight on, by approaching them with honesty. In a law practice, you're used to open disagreements. Just remember to focus on interests, not on positions.

The **passive-aggressive saboteurs** are a different story. They'll undercut you subtly outside your hearing. Their "support" will emphasize the "but" when they say "yes." Keep steering a straight course, emphasizing value and the Five Credos. It's hard to argue with participation in practice profitability.

The **silent minority** waits to see which way the wind is blowing. Each small step of progress that you make is a step toward winning them over. Share your successes willingly with them; even better, make *your* success *their* success.

The **eager puppies** embrace change for its own sake. They're only nominally allies – and they are too often written off by the more experienced members of the practice. Still, every voice raised in support is helpful.

The Leaders

There will be those who lead the movement toward Legal Project Management. They recognize the value it will bring to them and to their business – in this case, the practice of law. They understand that Legal Project Management is not an end in itself; rather, LPM is a tool – one of many – to enable a practice to provide improved service to its clients.

Provide value, control costs, offer predictability, and respond better to unplanned events. That's the gist of Legal Project Management. It's straightforward stuff, really, with a bit of new nomenclature.

Time to get started. As Willie the Shake says, you'll find a benefit in this change.

You shall find a benefit in this change.
William Shakespeare, *Antony and Cleopatra*

Index

Sources and Further Reading

Allen, D. (2001). *Getting Things Done: The Art of Stress-Free Productivity.* New York, NY: Viking Penguin.

Anderson, D., & Anderson, L. A. (2001). *Beyond Change Management: Advanced Strategies for Today's Transformational Leaders.* San Francisco, CA: Jossey-Bass.

Berkun, S. (2008). *Making Things Happen: Mastering Project Management.* Sebastapol, CA: O'Reilly Media.

Berkun, S. (2007). *The Myths of Innovation.* Sebastapol, CA: O'Reilly Media.

Berman, K., Knight, J., & Case, J. (2006). *Financial Intelligence: A Manager's Guide to Knowing What the Numbers Really Mean.* Boston, MA: Harvard Business Press.

Blanchard, K. H., & Johnson, S. (1982). *The One Minute Manager.* New York: Morrow.

Brooks, J. F. (1995). *The Mythical Man-Month: Essays on Software Engineering* (Second Edition ed.). Reading, MA: Addison-Wesley.

Buckley, J. R. (2005, January, March, April). Lawyerland (Welcome to Lawyerland; Adventures in Lawyerland; Escape From Lawyerland). *ACC Docket*, pp. 23-32; 78-84; 58-77.

Chandler, M. (2007, November 7). *Mark Chandler: 'I don't know a big company that isn't doing something'.* Retrieved July 18, 2009, from Times Online: http://business.timesonline.co.uk/tol/business/law/article2812342.e ce (or http://bit.ly/Lexician1075)

Chesler, E. R. (2009, January 12). Kill the Billable Hour. *Forbes*.

Cohen, A. R., & Bradford, D. L. (2005). *Influence Without Authority* (Second Edition ed.). New York, NY: J. W. Wiley and Sons.

Covey, S. R. (1989). *The 7 Habits of Highly Effective People: Powerful Lessons in Personal Change.* New York, NY: Free Press.

Darley, J. M., Teger, A. L., & Lewis, L. D. (1973). Do Groups Always Inhibit Individuals' Responses to Potential Emergencies? *Journal of Personality and Social Psychology*, *26*(3), 395-399.

Davis, J. B. (2009, October 7). *Jeffrey Carr: Playing With Aces.* Retrieved October 12, 2009, from ABA Journal's Legal Rebels -

Remaking the Profession:
http://www.legalrebels.com/posts/playing_with_aces/ (or
http://bit.ly/Lexician1074)

Fisher, R., & Ury, W. L. (1991). *Getting to Yes: Negotiating Agreement Without Giving In* (2nd ed.). New York, NY: Penguin.

Frederick P. Brooks, J. (1975). *The Mythical Man-Month: Essays on Software Engineering.* Reading, MA: Addison-Wesley.

Galbenski, D., & Barringer, D. (2009). *Unbound: How Entrepreneurship is Dramatically Transforming Legal Services Today* .

Gause, D. C., & Weinberg, G. M. (1989). *Exploring Requirements: Quality Before Design.* New York, NY: Dorset House.

Goffee, R., & Jones, G. (2009). *Clever: Leading Your Smartest, Most Creative People.* Cambridge, MA: Harvard Business School Press.

Greaves, W. (2006, August 29). *Ferrari Pit Stop Saves Alexander's Life.* Retrieved November 4, 2009, from Telegraph (UK): http://www.telegraph.co.uk/news/1527497/Ferrari-pit-stop-saves-Alexanders-life.html (or http://bit.ly/Lexician1073)

Hamel, G., & Breen, B. (2007). *The Future of Management.* Boston, MA: Harvard Business School Press.

Horvitz, E., & Apacible, J. (2003, November 7). *Learning and Reasoning About Interruption.* Retrieved May 22, 2009, from Microsoft Research: http://research.microsoft.com/en-us/um/people/horvitz/iw.pdf (or http://bit.ly/Lexician1072)

Klastorin, T. (2004). *Project Management: Tools and Trade-Offs.* New York, NY: John Wiley and Sons.

Kotter, J. P. (2008). *A Sense of Urgency.* Boston, MA: Harvard Business School Press.

Kotter, J. P. (1996). *Leading Change.* Boston, MA: Harvard Business School Press.

Kotter, J. P. (2002). *The Heart of Change: Real-Life Stories of How People Change Their Organizations.* Boston, MA: Harvard Business School Press.

Kouzes, J. M., & Posner, B. Z. (2002). *The Leadership Challenge.* San Francisco, CA: Jossey-Bass.

Kübler-Ross, E. (1969). *On Death and Dying.* New York, NY: MacMillan.

Lawyers as Accidental Project Managers. (2006, February). Retrieved November 4, 2009, from Morris, Manning & Martin: http://www.mmmlaw.com/articles/article_318.pdf (or http://bit.ly/Lexician1076)

Levy, S. B. (2009, July). The ABCs of KM. *ILTA White Papers: Knowledge Management - More Than the Sum of its Parts* , pp. 4-7.

Levy, S. B. (2007, May). The Ten-Minute Legal-Pro MBA. *ILTA White Papers: Finance Dollars and Sense* , pp. 4-6.

Lientz, B. P., & Rea, K. P. (1999). *Breakthrough Technology Project Management.* New York, NY: Academic Press.

Martin, R. (2007). *The Opposable Mind.* Boston, MA: Harvard Business School Press.

McConnell, S. (1998). *Software Project Survival Guide: How to Be Sure Your First Important Project Isn't Your Last.* Redmond, WA: Microsoft Press.

Moore, G. A. (2005). *Dealing With Darwin: How Great Companies Innovate at Every Phase of Their Evolution.* New York, NY: Portfolio/Penguin.

Moore, G. A. (2000). *Living on the Fault Line: Managing for Shareholder Value in the Age of the Internet.* New York, NY: Harper Business.

Morrison, R. (2009, September 23). *On my bucket list, ten metrics about outside counsel spend I hope I learn eventually.* Retrieved September 23, 2009, from Law Department Management: http://www.lawdepartmentmanagementblog.com/law_department _management/2009/09/on-my-bucket-list-ten-metrics-about-outside-counsel-spend-i-hope-i-learn-eventually.html (or http://bit.ly/Lexician1070)

Morrison, R. (2009). *Outside Counsel Management by Law Departments.* Princeton, NJ.

Muir, R. (2009, October 21). *What the New Law Firm Looks Like.* Retrieved October 21, 2009, from Robin Rolfe Resources: http://www.robinrolferesources.com/index.php?option=com_conten t&task=view&id=2561&Itemid=104 (or http://bit.ly/Lexician1071)

Oshry, B. (1994). *In the Middle.* Boston, MA: Power and Systems.

Oshry, B. (1999). *Leading Systems: Lessons From the Power Lab.* San Francisco, CA: Berrett-Koehler Publishers.

Oshry, B. (1996). *Seeing Systems: Unlocking the Mysteries of Organizational Life.* San Francisco, CA: Berrett-Koehler Publishers.

Oshry, B. (1992). *The Possibilities of Organization.* Boston, MA: Power and Systems.

Parkinson, C. N. (1957). *Parkinson's Law.* Boston: Houghton Mifflin.

Patterson, K., Grenny, J., McMillan, R., & Switzler, A. (2002). *Crucial Conversations: Tools for Talking When Stakes Are High.* New York: McGraw Hill.

Peters, T. J., & Waterman, R. H. (2004). *In Search of Excellence: Lessons From America's Best-Run Companies.* New York, NY: Harper.

Pfeffer, J. (2007). *What Were They Thinking? Unconventional Wisdom About Management.* Boston, MA: Harvard Business School Press.

Pigors, P., & Pigors, F. (1961). *Case Method in Human Relations: The Incident Method.* New York, NY: McGraw Hill.

Poppendieck, M., & Poppendieck, T. (2003). *Lean Software Development.* Boston, MA: Addison-Wesley.

Project Management Institute. (2008). *A Guide to the Project Management Book of Knowledge (PMBOK Guide)* (4th Edition ed.). Project Management Institute.

Scott, S. (2004). *Fierce Conversations: Achieving Success at Work and Life One Conversation at a Time.* New York, NY: Berkley Trade.

Scott, S. (2009). *Fierce Leadership: A Bold Alternative to the Worst "Best" Practices of Business Today.* New York, NY: Broadway Business.

Senge, P. M. (2006). *The Fifth Discipline: The Art & Practice of the Learning Organization.* New York, NY: Broadway Business.

Senge, P., Kleiner, A., Roberts, C., Smith, B., & Ross, R. (1994). *The Fifth Discipline Fieldbook: Strategies and Tools for Building a Learning Organization.* New York, NY: Doubleday.

Shaara, M. (1974). *The Killer Angels: A Novel of the Civil War.* New York, NY: Ballantine Books.

Shakespeare, W. (1623). *First Folio.* Retrieved from Internet Shakespeare Editions: http://internetshakespeare.uvic.ca

Smith, D. K. (1997). *Taking Charge of Change: Ten Principles for Managing People and Performance.* Boulder, CO: Perseus Publishing.

Standish Group. (2005). *Chaos Rising.* West Yarmouth, MA: Standish Group International.

Surowiecki, J. (2004). *The Wisdom of Crowds.* New York, NY: Bantam Dell.

Susskind, R. (2009). *The End of Lawyers? Rethinking the Nature of Legal Services.* New York, NY: Oxford University Press (USA).

Verzuh, E. (1999). *The Fast Forward MBA in Project Management: Quick Tips, Speedy Solutions, Cutting-Edge Ideas.* New York, NY: John Wiley and Sons.

Whitmore, J. (2002). *Coaching for Performance: Growing People, Performance, and Purpose* (Third Edition ed.). London, UK: Nicholas Brealey Publishing.

Wilterding, J., & Baughn, C. C. (1997). The Incident Process: A Case in Reverse. *Developments In Business Simulation and Experiential Learning , 24,* 320-321.

Young, M., & Gillies, J. (2009, September 17). What Lawyers Want. *KM Legal , 3* (6), pp. 25-26.

About the Author

Steven Levy is a technologist and project manager turned businessperson who has spent many years helping the legal world deliver increased value to clients.

He headed the legal technology department at Microsoft for many years, driving innovation and efficiency into one of the world's largest corporate law departments. He also led two industry task forces, served on the LEDES committee, and founded a corporate-law roundtable for sharing operations and technology information.

Also in his 17 years at Microsoft, he was a Principal Consultant in Microsoft Consulting Services, managed development of Microsoft's largest IT systems, and led multiple Microsoft product groups. Prior to joining Microsoft, he spent 15 years developing commercial software solutions, consulting, and managing projects in a variety of fields.

He currently heads Lexician, where he helps law firms and law departments get value, savings, and rapid return on investment from their projects and technology. He is a highly requested speaker and seminar leader, and he writes regularly on legal topics.

He and his family divide their time between Seattle and Lopez Island, Washington.

Thus far, with rough and all-unable pen, our bending author hath pursued the story.
William Shakespeare, *Henry V*

21118151R00205

Made in the USA
San Bernardino, CA
06 May 2015